AF454173

THE
PRINCIPLES
OF
CREATION

TEJAS HIREMANI

The Principles of Creation

Hardcover ISBN: 978-93-340-7369-0

All rights reserved.
No parts of this publication may be reproduced,
stored in a retrieval system, or transmitted, in any form or by
any means, electronic, mechanical, photocopying, recording,
or otherwise, without the prior permission of the author.

© Tejas Hiremani

Published by Callandor
Cover Design by Ronald Cruz (cruzialdesigns)

Powered by
Pothi.com
http://pothi.com

Contents

Author's Note

The Principles of Creation was an offshoot of personal philosophical thought inspired to be penned down after reading certain works such as the Tao Te Ching, the Bhagavad Gita, and Meditations by Marcus Aurelius. Though an indirect influence might be present, I have attempted to write it from scratch, without bias, or assumptions made from any work.

The book has four separate parts and there is a unity in its final form. Due to its structure, readers may find the change in tone a bit jarring, especially on entering the Futures section. This is by design and is how the book was written to be experienced. It might be helpful to have a slightly slower reading pace upon reaching those sections. For the highly commended science fiction story, readers could directly go to "Deus Ex Machina", the second last chapter in the book.

Stylistically also the book has been written in a manner which, rather than offering direct methods of improvement, stimulates intellectual thought and introspection. In my view that subliminally leads to betterment over time automatically than trying the same by following a certain process.

Kind Regards,
Tejas

THE PRINCIPLES
OF CREATION

1. Spirit

To Struggle Is To Grow.
Man Is One With The Struggle.

This is the fundamental truth of not only humans, but all living beings. Even a plate with a culture of bacteria stays constant over decades until some environmental change is introduced. It is then the hardiest of the microbes or the ones most adaptable to the new clime survive and create a new culture with better traits.

It is rather counterintuitive to believe in this, for to the average man, one strives that one may not have to in future. But as 'eternal bliss' is described in a single moment, the human mind breezes through times of non-struggle. It is as if one streams through years of one's life before one begins a new struggle. Keeping the struggle alive is akin to constantly improving, perhaps in different facets of life.

Is there a particular method to assume struggle? Though there may be no formulaic path, one can pick any craft or assignment one chooses to excel in. Then there are various ways in which one can put in effort, consistently, to improve over a long period. One of the ways to do so is to take the struggle as a fun experience. This is how children learn to balance, or walk and run. When one enjoys the process, has fun and is amused by it, the struggle becomes non-existent and one does not even feel the effort. To such a person, life is enormous pleasure and continuing existence a thrill. This is akin to the Taoist's way of non-doing doing. To be more precise for the above terms, it is effortless effort.

There are other ways to struggle and transform as well as we explore ahead.

Of great essence is it to realize that despite enormous efforts one may make and achieve mastery in a particular field, one can still be eclipsed by another who need make no effort for the same. A cheetah would be faster than any human being, however well trained, at a 100m race. A computer engine may after a few hours of training defeat the greatest grandmaster at chess. All struggle does is raise us from a natural plateau at one level to another at a higher level. There are and will be plateaus at a higher level than that, and at a lower level than our lowest. One who truly comprehends this can stay humble, however be his lot in life.

The walk that meanders through life can be associated with a shrinking rubber band. Though it has no real presence, a rubber band that shrinks reduces its size and contour and proclivity to stretch as time flows forward. The hands that stretch the rubber band can increase its length, and its elasticity, so it may be stretched to surprising limits. They must be delicate hands, though, for at a particular moment, pull it too wide, and it may snap, and forever lose its inherent nature of a rubber band. If the hands do not apply the stretch regularly, the rubber band will become smaller and smaller and lose more elasticity than it had gained. But the hands that are consistent in their pull, and careful, that rubber band can be elongated to unexpected and fearsome lengths!

Unfortunately, man is not given over twenty-four hours every day. Innumerable attractive options present themselves – they titillate, entice, and enchant in potential and effect. From martial arts to flourishes of the paintbrush, social upheavals to probes of mathematical statements, physicians to culinary delights, choices abundant thrive in the vast sphere of potentialities. Practicality dictates one can but pursue a few of them to mastery. How then can one select one's path among the plenteous? Does one consider the incessant whispering of the brain or the importunate chatter of fellow people, or innate ability and skill? Or is there a more powerful call, a mystic force of pure nature drawn from within, that seizes the self, that propels one, and guides true, even if one proceeds ahead with eyes bound and ears halted?

2. Freedom

Live From The Heart

A seed, as it sprouts, raises its stem towards the sky, while its roots dig inward into the ground. There is no innate intelligence that dictates its position, orientation, or transformation into a tree. It is simply the nature of the seed, formed through billions of years of evolution. In work, or plans, we usually make decisions based on directions given by a relatively new organ on the evolutionary tree – the brain. Our heart, comparatively, and the impulses that come with it are far more ancient. Some may be unintuitive, we might impute a level of silliness to others, and follow a few more without much thought.

Upon gathering the acts of man, one can recognize that logic is but a slave used to explain away our primal deeds rather than a master that dictates them. Most of man's actions - the absorption of a trade, the composition of a song or poem, romantic overtures, going to war, rearing children - are those set forth by the heart of a free man. The mind does have a role in their success, but it is the heart that directs. For if one only took decisions based on cold calculations, one would be more successful, perhaps, but it would be a bland life, a monotonous one, without passionate enterprise.

In all labour, the concordance of the individual to the efforts undertaken has the utmost power. It is true in previous ages coercion has been used to produce goods or construct immense structures. But in all such cases, the human being is no better than a mindless beast. He does as told without thought, without input, simply exerting the energy required and moving his muscles in predetermined paths. The requirement is only at a surface layer in him; his inner body and mind are focused elsewhere (perhaps on a good hot meal). Turn away the whips, allow for individual freedom, and an astonishing advance of ideas bursts forth, potentially giving an output far more than was envisaged. Individual freedom and exploration created inventions like the wheel, the sewing machine and the printing press.

More than brute force, it is effective to explain through details of why a particular task is of importance and its broader consequences, or its attractiveness and beauty. An individual who concurs with this, and then does a task of his own free will, is as a self-taught person instead of one who does it regarding it to be a chore.

The finest artists, be it at the piano, or poetry, or play, are honed by an innate persistence to improve. Love, perhaps inexplicable, forever indomitable, can have us reach that unknown enchanted region that slakes individual desire and yet stokes divine fervour. That which comes from the heart is an effort of individual sinews, spirit, and soul.

To love, though, brings challenges unexpected and daunting. The parable ahead serves an illustration.

Years ago lived there a modest peasant who grew strawberries on a small strip of land. The peasant was slim, with a mindful nature, and nurtured his crops carefully. When the time to reap came, he and his wife would pick lush reddened strawberries, full and ripe, off the field, and fill their baskets with it. In the evening, by the warm wind that brought the fragrance of the fruits, beside the fortifying streams of the river, they would part their mouths and moisten their lips with sweet savour. The birds chirped, the green grass swayed either way and their bellies slowly warmed and sated with provision. And they were content.

In the same area lived there a lord. And this lord was large, and he had a thick mane of hair, and was of a proud bearing. And the lord would hold a banquet every week that had troves of items on the menu – salted pork, roast chicken, peas and pies, potato stews, bread and broth, dollops of wine, and generous drink. The lord would lustfully chew on the offerings, and between bouts of loud discussion, pour flagons of agitated liquid past his throat. But the lord felt weary, and overcome, and barely tasted the sumptuous meals, and he would be stricken with aches, worry, tense exchanges with his advisors, and, worst of all, indigestion. And during his rounds, the lord would notice the peasant and wonder at his even temperament.

And one day the lord accosted the peasant and asked him, 'You have neither money nor land nor does good food fall into your hand. Pray then, tell me, how is it you stay content with your meagre possessions, while I, a lord, having available every luxury, am wracked with all manner of affliction?'

The peasant replied, 'I have not much. But of what I do have, I sense fully. I taste dear every morsel, and every bite of food I get. I am invigorated by the warmth of the sun, feel refreshed when the rains come, and a breeze surrounds me. The fragrance of the fruits I grow and the smell of the fertile soil soothes me, and I wish for no more. Not fancy drink, nor an array of servants, nor golden possessions. If I did get them, I would not say nay, I want them not. Mayhap the lords be happy with their treasures and their lands. But I am content as I stand. I am wrought as is my measure.'

To this the lord contemplated gravely. And as his thoughts coalesced into comprehension, he declared, 'Then a curse it is to be rich! For we lords plot ceaselessly that one may gain more prestige than the other. My own servants I cannot trust not to spy on me or betray me for coin. The king's eye is on my land – there is a plot he has lain his desires upon! Can I take delight in delicacies or lavish in luxuries? You can avail yourself the pleasures of your station far more than I can! No one befriends you for their benefit, for you have nothing to give! And no one would betray you for the same reason! But I, I am important, I am burdened with power! And yet all these riches and titles are powerless to grant me my one desire – a mind at peace! Does not society then deceive man – have him pursue lofty ambitions, and even attain them, only to be denied the pleasure of their success?'

The peasant too spent several moments in deep thought, and then said humbly, 'It may be society deceives not, but does so out of the goodness of its heart. Would not any man say one is blessed if one does not have to scurry around for food or shelter? Perhaps society lacks the capacity to perceive that relief from basic wants does not assure us a relaxed mind. However, I believe society is nascent yet. For does not everyone deserve peace within, be he poor or rich, child or elderly, man or woman? And in future society may offer a pattern, or a method, which if followed, could grant us that elusive rascal – Peace!'

3. Karma

The Source Of All Problems In The World
Is Unfairness Or Perceived Unfairness

All revolutions, rebellions, wars, and revolts in the world are due to a perception of unfairness in relations between two groups. When people have listened to the other group, and altered relations to be fairer, much sorrow and conflict have been averted, while when they have used power to keep the other group in misery, in servitude, or others have taken advantage of weakness and leniency, the result has almost always been calamitous.

A case in point is that of Russian serfs. There was serfdom in Russia for centuries, where serfs, or laborers, were bonded to their landlords. They were not allowed to travel, and could not work for anyone but their own landlord. The Russian tsars tried to abolish serfdom to lessen their burden, but the feudal lords kept the serfs in debt, and thus servitude, for their entire lives. What followed was a failed revolution in 1905, then a successful one in 1917, and then yet another to overthrow the imperialists who had overthrown the tsar, then a bloody Civil War and famine with unimaginable suffering. Indeed at this point the people so distrusted the nobility and landowners that they disavowed capitalism and attempted a society based on communism, or communal ownership of property. That which could have been averted by allowing people to freely choose their livelihood and have landlords compete for labour!

A person who allows for genuine satisfaction among the people by a pervading sense of fairness builds his identity as a leader. A just leader reaches the hearts of his people.

Fairness is an individual perspective. A lion deems it unfair to go hungry while tasty deer roam the plains. When a lion hunts deer, the deer gives up its life, while the lion has only had a single meal.

In most cases, monetary compensation or appropriate recognition are sufficient to be fair rewards for an individual's efforts. Only violence has been the exception to this rule. Blood has been paid for with more blood.

Unfairness may extend for a long stretch of time. It is a man with a steady and firm will who keeps a balanced mind and refrains from attempting an unmeasured response when circumstances are against him for a long while. If he does not lose faith and stays steadfast in his efforts, he would eventually reap the fruits he has long sought.

Those who have persevered with their belief in the right way despite being unfairly treated for a long period of time – such as freedom fighters – are the great souls of the world.

What is karma? It emerges from the notion of 'fairness' possessed by every individual – the sense one has that good deeds have corresponding rewards and bad ones determine a commensurate amount of suffering. The idea is encapsulated in karma as a tabulation of accrued 'debt' of sorts that is due to be cleared in time. According to the law of karma, actions – good or bad – are not isolated incidents which can be contained after their occurrence but their effects ripple across the fabric of spacetime and originate a 'counter' action, or reaction, or response, to neutralise the 'iniquity visited' from the original action.

Amongst other meanings, karma is the intrinsic tendency of existence to correct past occurrences of unfairness by a *reversal* of roles among the oppressor and the oppressed. If unchecked, society can continually oscillate between such occurrences of unfairness – a hand for a hand, limb for limb. Which is why forgiveness is so powerful: it breaks the eternal cycle of karma itself!

Those whose cause is motivated by karma have the power of righteousness in them.

4. Dharma

What Causes Unhappiness In A Person?

It is because one has an absolute in one's mind and then a contrary event occurs. For instance, if one believes he must be promoted at the end of the year, and his mind absolutely refuses to consider the possibility that it may not happen, and he is not promoted, then he is unhappy. Or if someone has a definite way in which he expects others to behave and another does not behave of the same accord, it causes unhappiness.

Desire, or attachment to a degree is not harmful *per se*, as long as it does not overwhelm the being completely.

However, one can be absorbed totally in the *process* of achieving one's betterment in craft, or disposition.

To reduce malcontent in the world and encourage harmony, partly directly through sages, prophets and mystics, and partly organically through societal structures and customs, codes of behaviour were adopted. They have various appellations: Dharma in Hinduism, The Way, The Code, Justice, Honour, Tradition, Ethics, Asha. Those who transgress these rules are punished that injustice may not consume society!

There may be more than a single defined path one can follow and keep one's peace with social order. And these paths are ever-changing, intermingling, smooth, rough with obstacles, and new ones may be formed! Only when we venture far beyond into dark ways shunned by civilization is the stability of society threatened. And here the immortal law of karma begins its long reach – it takes note of the injustices that occur, and seeks to correct them. In consequence, it overcompensates with further injustices.

Picture a see-saw fixed in place above the sea. Dharma has it balanced: it prevents either end from dipping into the sea water. When injustice rises in the world, one end dips into the water of disharmony, and then the force of karma unleashes its inexorable pull and causes the entire apparatus to swing, dip in one end once, and then the other repeatedly. Only when a new set of laws is introduced, or mode of living, or constitution acceptable to the majority and abreast with the time, has the magnitude of the movement been sufficiently reduced to get it back to an equilibrium.

A person who follows a given dharma in his field is given that incomparable and priceless quality – confidence.

Social harmony brought about by dharma is but a precursor to he who constitutes society – the individual. And the individual is beholden to society if harmony is yet to be brought forth. But upon the establishment of a settlement, man may rightfully ask, 'What of my person?' And the question begs the answer.

5. Purpose

What Is That Which Is Most Important
For Any Individual? Duty

The idea of duty goes far beyond that which arises from normal human establishments. It can be traced back to the origin of life itself, when differing proteins in cells began to have specialized functions that kept the cell alive and healthy. Then rose clusters of cells which started having varying roles to keep the unit at an optimal level. As multicellular organisms emerged, groups of animals formed with some playing the role of protectors, some to feed, some to nurture, etc. Any effort made in the furtherance of one's task is the fulfilment of eons of moulding of the human soul. This lends one the enormous satisfaction upon spending a day immersed in productive work.

Deeds that lead the community to progress are ones mankind is drawn to. Through practice in one's efforts, one's output in nature starts to be distinctive and clearer and takes shape as a unique identity to oneself which when viewed from the union to the individual, can be discerned as Purpose.

The singular element of life is that of Purpose. Without it, life is a wanton construction of a flurry of meaningless activity, and reality merely a haphazard collection of occurrences that continue to happen – the mindless wanderings of a bunch of particles. Why would one wake up and confront the day with methodical intent were it not for an underlying purpose? For man can ingest the necessary nutrients, perform daily tasks, avoid dangerous situations and gain small pleasures in hobbies, gatherings and soothing activities and whittle away a drab life characterized by unfulfilled promise. Or man could focus immense energies on that which engulfs, penetrates, feasts, consumes and electrifies the universe!

Dharma lends balance to the collective. Purpose grants strength to the individual.

One who has a directed purpose has the force of determination in him. It is the unquenchable fire, the reserved will that creates, sustains and fortifies life.

A particular belief of legend has it man, before birth, is imbued with a distinctive purpose. And afore he is pulled into the world, perception of his being is wiped from his mind. For what would life promise, or excite with possibilities, if man were aware of the precise nature of his bodily existence? As routine and random experiences progress, it may strike man in a thunderous instant or through a gradual formulation – but then his purpose is laid bare and the breadth of his nature crystallizes before him for the necessity of his trials and his vast part in the cosmos.

Is all then as fate so chooses? Or do a person's decisions and desires, abilities, unwavering exertions, and the tremendous application of an implacable will change the course of one's set path? Perhaps destiny is malleable, and fluctuating, as the winds, and perhaps our part in the world does influence destiny laid down by the unseen immaterial. Or is destiny inextricably entwined with our deeds and works, the one causing the other, and the other in turn directing the one, as two strands of DNA that twist and thrust, and yet mould a definite sense of the living?

6. Mortality

All Creatures Have Simple And Basic Needs, And Those Needs Are – Food And Sex

Despite being enormously complex, the human being too is instinctively driven to satisfy natural urges. They are created by evolution: any organism first tries to achieve sustenance for itself and when that is successful, it seeks to breed and create more of its kind. After all, if it did not, its line would die out, and others who did not follow this pattern would remain.

It is said a young man, after much pondering, put forth the following uncontested assertion:

'We are born. We die.'

And after several years, and studies, and conversations with many learned men and women, he became a mature philosopher. Subsequently he modified his original statement as so:

'We are born. We reproduce. And we die.'

And the man then regarded his work fulfilled.

One can add another very enigmatic need to the mix, and that is sleep. Food, sex, and sleep are the holy trinity that complete a creature's wants. Sleep is the most mysterious of the three, and why it is needed at all is a subject of research unto itself.

A startling fact to note is that we, in our characteristic fashion, have wrought an analogous metric to gauge progress of a civilization. The gross domestic product, which is considered the size of wealth of a nation, corresponds to the drive to feed. It initially began as a measure of the agricultural produce, and then widened to include goods and services as a whole. In the future, it will assimilate virtual goods. However, this all-encompassing metric is but a shadow of the platonic ideal of food. It is but a feverish wrapping around the happenstance of monkeys scampering to collect more items, more material, in the phantasm that they would not go hungry if they had enough. What it misses completely is the second natural drive, that of sex.

Sex it is that great personas have undergone – a consummate yet untouched realization – without being aware of it. The attainment of a bliss beyond that of a full belly. What exactly is the shadow cast by the platonic fire of sex? To answer this once more we need to delve into our evolutionary past.

To produce better offspring, mates must be selected with capabilities unseen in others. And that one may copulate with such a mate, one is given a heightened sense of rapture for the act. Proceeding which successive generations, through ongoing competition, seek to enhance those very capabilities. Thus came into being the colourful extravagant plumage of a peacock.

As the immediate need for nourishment was taken care of, and man was allowed thoughts unencumbered, mates started enjoying more time, often having deeper relationships, with those who reached a higher level in a particular skill.

And then, just as kindled fire is no longer described as a pack of logs which combust in an exothermic reaction, but acquires an identity of its own – that of fire – so too did artistic forms emerge from our sexual natures to be independent entities pursued for their own sake.

Reaching the pinnacle of an artistic endeavour brings about an enduring contentment. Every scientific advancement, every story written or poem sung, every musical piece or painting, every mathematical truth uncovered, every time man has set out to explore new lands, seas or mountains, every sporting achievement, every product built with finesse and unmatched detail – all germinate from the sexual instinct, but are no longer beholden to it. They are but manifestations of the human sexual spirit. And, without being aware of it, whether it be wrestling or soccer, painting or modelling or dancing, all art forms are displays of fertility! An enormous cry to the world that one's body is primed and ready, that a distinctive flesh is available to be sought out and coveted!

The artistic streak is that which leads to experimentation, as well as unexpected yet pleasing outcomes.

Though distinct from sex, every art form still stays faithful to its rudimentary structure. It begins with a certain tension, a conflict and an uncertainty of path, then has rising and falling periods of excitement, wonder and strife and culminates in a fitful climax, followed by a post coital temporary release from the coils of existence.

7. The Truth

Beyond The Wellspring Of The Visual World, The Truth Beckons

Six principles manifest in all creatures, but the appeal to the truth draws one who reaches a higher level in both consciousness and thought. As humans, we eventually are drawn not to rumours, or opinions, or unconfirmed reports, but to actuality, to essence. It is the desire for truth that raises and separates us from baser, and more instinctive, creatures.

At a higher plane are Seekers of the Truth. For above all, it is indelible. Infallible. Absolute. That which can neither be denied nor questioned. And yet unassuming, quiet, potent. Which, upon common assumption is the potentate that unifies mankind.

At the pinnacle of their reach, all thoughts, words, philosophies and resolutions are directed towards the same goal.

A reconciliation. An encapsulation. The *raison d'etre*. Clarity. To unearth, refine and polish from the whirrings of chaos the Eternal Way in its sublimity, its fullness and its supreme elegance.

Truth is the expression of existence.

In a manner subtle, relaxed, playful, it envelops the tentative grope of the mind. The laws of physics, which in their munificence explain the governance of the smallest particles to the galaxies, are core tenets of the truth.

Zoom into the atomic and sub-atomic region, and particles can, counterintuitively, be in multiple places at the same time, and can communicate instantaneously with each other. This is the quantum realm, where they are nought but waves extending across space – in flux, untamed, and quivering. It is only when we measure them are they made corporeal and brand themselves in a definite spot. Of myriad possibilities, the particle leaves an exact imprint of itself on the fabric of reality, which is, finally, the truth! Of all possibilities, the one that actually happened. A continuation of the grand story of the cosmos, at the tiniest of bearings, borne forth by light.

As water flows, it collects and deposits material, and thereby moves information about matter. It has a pure quality, for water pushes forth equally, accepts all matter, and in a neutral fashion, thrusts particles across the world. Likewise, light carries information about particles throughout the universe. The difference is it does not carry the particles themselves! Its form is that of pure energy, which traverses space at the fastest speed possible. Massless, that which cannot be held, unsurpassed in speed, and which describes without bias the unfolding story of matter.

Light captures the flow of the universe. Without light, the universe isn't just dark, for in the absence of observation, it does not exist! It is the purity of light that records the justification of existence. The creation of the universe is co-eval with as was told in a wise phrase – 'Let there be light!'

'Let there be light!' came the summons, and thus was darkness created.

On the powers that command the motions of large bodies, it is the weakest of the forces – gravity – that exerts an influence over the immense distances of space. Such power is wrought by it, that a sufficiently massive body can collapse in itself and form a bottomless pit, inescapable, from which not even light can emerge. The black hole, then, holds the secrets of the universe as that which the light leaves cannot be kept secret. Truth is thus intimately connected with secret, for every secret needs the truth to become one, every secret has a truth it does not yield, but truth has that which may or may not be secret – and to it they are both the same.

Is that which is absorbed and digested by a black hole unsalvageable? Despite its gargantuan hold, just as the tiny force of gravity compounded has great impact, it is the microscopic – the quantum arena whose mystic workings defy conventional notions of physics – which lets information amassed within the black hole leak without. The truth is there, the truth permeates, but whether the truth can be unravelled, streamlined and consolidated – that may perhaps be left to a higher order.

Were we to probe to the uttermost depths though, the truth is incomprehensible and intangible as the perfect but unattainable regions of mathematical assertions. Once mathematics is applied to actual life it reduces to merely a poor and crude approximation of what previously was exact and glorious symmetry. That is Plato's World where lie all the perfections and ideals that can be thought of. There lies every mathematical statement unblemished, the best stories that could be told, the most sensible decisions to have been taken in every crisis, the perfect romance, Beethoven's 10th Symphony, and even competent politicians!

The truth is but sullied by our perusal. The real truth is unreachable. And being unreachable, it becomes a thing of fascination but lacks surety as to its usefulness. As the beginning of the Tao Te Ching says, 'The Tao (way) that can be spoken is not the true Tao. The name that can be named is not the true name'.

Though only humans relate to the truth, having the intellectual bent, it is the integral principal which, from the bare to the overarching, conceives and weaves the world. It would be improper to state in our hubris – impudently – that it serves to assuage the curiosities of our aristocratic fancies, for those who seek alike with the living, the non-living, and the particulate are not but beholden to the immortal laws, but veritable expositions of them. Past instinctive creatures, simpler organisms, microscopic beings – the principle at the minuscule yet applies to all in equal measure, despite awareness of it rising as mental ability does. Can we say it belongs not to those with lesser a developed logical reach if they are a portrait of further an incipient cause? That which acts at the smallest, most elementary of levels is pursued by the higher of beings.

A disciple of the truth stays analytical, objective, and tries to be unbiased. In response, or equivalently, due the focused effort, he has a sense of calm in and around his self. At the beginning we mentioned there are different ways to tackle struggle. Each principle described fashions a new way, and state of mind, for the challenge.

Lastly as investigative thoroughness requires, one may ask – what quality has the truth that so attracts? Why does the truth have an allure that causes an abandonment of routine, a usurpation of individual faculty, and a dedication of consummate ability that escapes momentary distraction?

For those with a stout grasp on the rules that ordain behaviour, rational thought and decisions can enhance well-being and further a better survival rate. The understanding of crop growth and soil fertility propelled man to break through the population barriers due his previous nomadic torpor. Iron smelting and metal casting lent him an edge in the warrior age which came about inevitably. Accurate details of a crime allow for the dispensation of justice, and thence promote social harmony. The precise description of phenomena provided by reliable witnesses presents an optimal action to be taken for advancement. But this rationale hardly scratches the elemental layer, the outer shell of the reason for our preoccupation with the truth. For in it the truth is no different than other equally significant principles and their call to our exertions.

Is it related to the emergence of thought? Thoughts begin with observation and end in closure. A thought loop is the final resolution of the thought – the observation, the question, the understanding, and the solution which establishes harmony between the beginning and the end. Though the thought loop be set aside as a redeemed unit, further thoughts may arise from it. Invariably, an inquisitive mind asks why, and, as the string of questions streams on, one question is etched more so than others – why is there a why? To question the question. Thence a single answer outstrips competing ones – The Answer. A thought loop quietens and sates an unruly reckoning. The more penetrative and insightful the question, the grander the settlement registers and the further the depth of the satiety. To wit, there looms on the edge of our hand outstretched the most profound sense of the most influence and of balance – The Ultimate Answer – which once attained or imbibed eliminates for ever more the need or rise of uncertainty or doubt and ensures tranquillity everlasting.

The instinct to pursue and rectify a thought is but a consequence of the evolutionary medium. This serves as the middle layer in the quest to understand the truth that captivates. It does explain the need of a level of intelligence and why intelligent beings would expend efforts in furtherance of the truth. But it yet fails to elevate the truth to the plane of the exalted, for its basis, albeit powerful, is but among other instincts developed from evolution as the need for shelter, the search for mates, and complex social engagements.

What then? At the deepest layer, the truth speaks to the innermost core that has existed in us since we first gathered sufficient organic molecules to be deemed animate. A secret longing, partially explained, and gradually explicable as the potential to express feelings grows with anatomic complexity essays the urgent craving bound within. It is that desire that prompts such behaviour, sometimes inexplicable, as sacrifice, as ancestor worship, as the moulding of idols to cast into sharp definition a muddy abstraction, as replete love given to an unknown entity. Taken to the end, these customs are clumsy yet innocent attempts to draw an image of the unquantifiable. To be as a whole, one with the limitless force. It is that which has even an oft repeated trope feel fresh. God. Enlightenment. The Awakening. Bliss Eternal and All Consuming. A Utopia constructed with the sweat of one's brow. To ride along the Elysian Fields. To enter bidden the Kingdom of God. To lay before the Face of Mankind – Paradise Unquenched. To Feast in Valhalla after Ragnarok. And at dusk ease into the sandy beaches of heaven and behold the golden sunset over the icy blue waves that foam the frigid ocean as the azure sky opens over softly melting glaciers. To sway, immerse, and flow in unison with the wondrous currents of the Eternal Tao. In the Apotheosis of Dance, enter a primeval trance in concordance with the Delicate Music of Brahman. After countless eons of search, to secure palpable the Fruit of Inner Peace. The Serenity of finding the Last Answer. A Boundless, Unmatched and Peerless Love – The Gift of Providence. Universal Consciousness. Nirvana.

With simple words, a tone of grace, of beauty, the truth is given access to the tremulous recesses of the soul. A resonant thirst that echoes through the ages – to gainsay that knowledge which can douse once and finally the fires of iniquity, of conflict. For in sufferance was genesis, and amidst great trials was born a semblance of the Civilization of Man. The truth promises nothing less than a vindication of the past. Of mysteries, immense and young, explanation. For hardship, recompense. Offered that which is broken, restoration. Given deeds, good and evil, fair judgement. And the future, hope. Not at the end of all things, but during the course of the treasured drop of life, offers it penitence for transgression, kindness towards the anguished, mercy to those who lapse, and affection for those forsaken. Harbours it the Key to the Original Testament that holds strong despite being battered by fearsome opposing winds that are but tenuous waves of air. For organisms that have been tossed, buffeted, whipped, and shoved relentlessly by the vagaries of cruel indifference, they can partake yet, and be replenished by, the fine wine of adaptability from the Chalice of Youth – a reprieve welcome. And gently descend onto solid firmament unchangeable. Held close to the Bosom of the Maker, a solemn covenant issues forth. A promise, ancient and venerated, of absolution, a clean and redolent province, that tends to the Bounteous Garden. One with bonds and shackles expunged. That shall render impotent the inescapable struggle to have arisen at the dawn of time. Where the brethren are provided nourishment as needed. Without command to decant the Warm Elixir of Triumph drawn bonafide from the meticulous admixture of the Peace Keepers. To be with the Harbinger, who heralds the utter defeat of death, disease, decay, and lament. To Be. Among the aroma of floral wreaths and eaves of the forest, to compact and reaffirm vehement the Immortal Seal Salubrious of Salvation that portends eternal rejuvenation and delivers from pain, from grief.

And thus, the circle is complete.

THE PAST –
THE ORIGIN OF LIFE

Love Was The First Emotion To Come Into Being. The Second Was Hate

Love has not always been the myriad of types we see and experience today. We are fortunate to behold romantic love, filial love, friendly love, possessive love, melancholic love, maternal love, patriotic love, community love and plenty more. But from whence did it arise? And was there a time it was in some primitive form, unmolested, even a blooming mixture of a hodgepodge of sentiments, one that would be unrecognizable as love today?

As we make our way to a particular location on earth, deep into the oceans, in the thermal vents of genesis, far far away into the protracted mists of the newly formed earth cooling to sanitary temperatures, witness would we a bundle of self-assembled chemicals. These chemicals could, under the right conditions, bring about similar chemicals into being from existing matter in the warm mixture of organic ingredients called 'primordial soup'. They were the progenitors of life forms – made propitiously persistent by a formative mode of reproduction. Since the chemicals had adaptable molecules, those molecules that enabled chemicals to duplicate faster, or more effectively given the surroundings, spread. Of this came the propensity to succour other beings – a nascent form of unconditional love. This was at a time much before even a rudimentary structure of a cell came about. Every part of a cell that keeps the cell alive and functioning, similar to every individual cell and organ that keeps an organism healthy, has in its innermost nature the same molecules. Love is not an outcome of their functional ways. We are love at our core constituents. And it is an unconditional love, equally directed at all living beings!

Love is the first of elementary responses to germinate in any evolutionary system, before even sentience or nociception.

Once organisms spread throughout an ecosystem, and competition began for resources, it was then that traits which gave an advantage to one organism or group of organisms over another started to emerge. These traits developed into what would today be recognized as a primitive form of hate. Hatred, like love, is a product of the evolution of life. It seeks the destruction of an opposing group so that static resources may be enjoyed by the former, thereby allowing it to breed and increase its populace.

However, hatred cannot stand as an independent entity in and of itself. If it did so, then once an opposing group was vanquished, the members within the group would turn on each other and fight until there was but a single individual left. And the single individual, being consumed with hatred, would not breed, as this would create a competitor. As a result, its line would die out.

Additionally, hate owes its existence to love. It is love that begets hate. For at this point during evolution, love is already established as a determining force. If we did not love our fellow mates, we would not fight to acquire land and resources for them from our enemies. Or if we did not love the self, composed of a multitude of cells, we would not challenge out another if he denigrated us!

The relevance and reach of evolution can be further taken to the tiniest particles – the swarm that constitutes reality. Smaller than bacteria, smaller than viruses, smaller even than atoms and molecules, are the basic constituents of matter: electrons, protons, and neutrons. If we take the electron, the muon and the tau, they are all similar fundamental particles, though the muon and tao are transient and decay very quickly. But just their occurrence dictates that circumstances and spatial conditions promote their sustenance for a very long time, by the standards of the shortest time period possible – the Planck time. No extra information or technique is required between survival of these elementary particles and the survival of organic molecules after genesis. So, the same force that powered the spread of organic life exists in the void and thrum of space too. Love is the most primitive, universal and elementary presence!

All Positive Emotions Stem From Love. Negative Ones Stem From Hatred

As life became more complex, so too did the emotions that guide and drive us. A cursory glance allows visualization into the staggering breadth of emotions in us – excitement, greed, anger, amusement, forgiveness, belonging, friendliness, teasing, etc. Despite their enormous diversity, we can trace their growth from the two basic emotions which arose during the genesis of life – love and hate. Positive emotions like care, forgiveness, humour, will, accommodation, sacrifice have their roots in love; while negative ones like anger, jealousy, pride, sloth, cruelty, malice do so in hate. A discerning view would distil out either love or hate from any emotion.

Calmness is the only exception, for it is the absence of any emotion, positive or negative. It is the zero, the point from whence other emotions can be observed. Calmness is as water – just as the earliest organisms were present, part of, and moved with the currents of the hot springs of genesis. They had no way to propel themselves, or adjust the environ to suit their needs – and they consisted mostly of water themselves! All they could, in their non-sensory way, do was observe and flow – just as the waters around them did.

The brain is the only organ that feels no pain or sensation, and yet its role is to observe the same through the rest of the body.

When viewed objectively from a calm origin naturally occurring rivalries, feelings and competencies that arise from hatred are managed by the establishment of norms and rules. That is the cause of codes of behaviour – dharma – and adherence to the correct ways prevents the spread of chaos or breakdown of society. Ironically, we owe the stability created by an order-bound society to the imbalance created by hate. There would be no rule or even the need for it were the world only composed of love.

Amor Vincit Omnia

Logic – rational and calculating thought – is a relatively new occurrence on the tree of life. It was not needed when life was mostly a struggle to seek out food, and avoid becoming food. The instinctive emotions of hunger and fear dictated those. Logic developed perhaps ten thousand years ago, which is a blink in the evolutionary timeline of 4 billion years.

When was the last time someone remembered a perfectly crafted logical argument? How many people talk about the internal consistency of a legal theory? Contrast this with when someone remembers one singing a song, or having a life-threatening moment. Events that evoke strong stirrings in one affect, motivate and lead. We are driven more by our emotions than by cold rational thought.

One has a choice in deciding by which emotions one lets oneself be taken. They will have their source in either love, or hate.

There are times when one has been affected, and made consequential decisions based on what would have an underlying current of hate. In the long term, this has almost always been disastrous, though it may be unstoppable for a short while. Eventually, it is only when through some chance collection of propitious ideas rooted in tones of amity, peaceable voices have prevailed, that a semblance of stability, of prosperity even, appeared.

Amor Vincit Omnia. Love conquers all.

As an example, consider the empires of Rome and Parthia, the largest empires of the ancient world. They had wars between each other for centuries, to no avail. Over the ages, both empires had comparable armies, weapons, and tactics. Their continuous warfare only sucked up resources, labour, and money which could have been used for welfare of the people. They fought each other to the ruin of both empires.

A case closer to our times, and that of a victor and loser, was World War I. At the end of the war, the Treaty of Versailles was aimed to punish and extract from Germany heavy reparations for the war, though Germany had simply come to the aid of its allies at the outbreak of the war. In the words of Winston Churchill, the victors wanted to 'squeeze it by the tits until the pips squeak'. As Germany was unable to fulfil the excessive demands heaped upon it, the severity of hardship the country underwent contributed to the rise of Nazism and World War II. When, at the close of the Second World War, the Allies chose their path, this time it was motivated by a more sensible approach. They provided support to rebuild the war-torn country. And the *Wirtschaftswunder*, the German economic miracle, precluded another war, and the economic strength the country achieved meant it could pay back far more than what usual post-war diktats deemed sufficient.

The hand that reaches out to another in friendship is favoured over a pen that condemns one to harsh judgement.

War Is Testosterone

The past consists of much magnificence, wonder, suffering, unexpected heroism and exceptional terror. It is enigmatic, spontaneous, unforeseeable and in a particular aspect, filled with violence, bloodletting, conflict and trauma. In the aggregate, they may be described in a loose word of a single syllable – war. Its plainness and allure are deceptive, for in war, human beings go forth into other lands with the intention to murder, loot, rape, destroy towns, and assemble resources for further conquest.

In all cases, armies have been comprised of men who have gone forth for plunder and mayhem. Our innate sexual natures dictate the directions we incline towards. A woman is not going to get more pregnant by going to war; on the contrary, the dangers and risk of bodily harm far reduce her chances of successfully having offspring. Even the time spent in waging war is valuable time she could have used during the limited period of her fertility, which is usually a couple of decades. What a woman needs for her reproductive wants is stability and the availability of resources and protection to raise her children.

Man is led by the ever-present swinging of a couple of seed producing, hormone injecting globules suspended lightly in an unobtrusive sack with multiple folds.

Before the Age of Empires, many millennia ago, there was no war. There were no weapons, beyond sharpened sticks and stones. Resources were plentiful for the lower population of the times. War was harmful for groups coexisting in the same lands, as it would simply reduce their populations unnecessarily.

When the population started to exceed what could be supported by the lands – then – began war. And it was man who gradually got more and more organised and went on conquest. For a victorious man gains land and resources and women by which he can selectively propagate his genes to future generations, and give them the upbringing, training, and ability to further propagate theirs.

The male of any species produces enough sperm to inseminate all receptive females upon release. The male gamete is particularly abundant in nature, and fierce competition, which may be violent, decides the victorious male who gains breeding rights. Males of some species of deer lock antlers and struggle with each other until the winner severely wounds the other. The winner then gets to copulate with female deer, propagating the very genes that brought about victory. A male lion spends his life fending off challenges to his harem from other attacking males. A male elephant in musth goes off on a violent frenzy that cannot be controlled. During musth, its testosterone level may be 60 or more times that of its normal level! And while infused with the stimulating molecule, it can inflict much damage on surrounding males, and people, but also receives excited calls from nearby females in heat.

Man is but a repository of sperm.

A woman is the womb that nurtures life.

Much of a male's reproductive success is related to violent removal of competitive sperm, and consequently, ingrained in the sexual hormone itself – testosterone.

When we consider war, it is but male tendency towards violence, seeded by testosterone, furthered by man's ability to organize into fighting units, and made concrete by the multiple resources gained, encouraging more males into the business.

At its core, war is testosterone. It is an amplification of man's sexual drive on an empire wide scale.

37

A Larger Population Reduces The Chances of War

Paradoxically, the larger the population gets, the lesser it may be that war would occur in a given region.

When armies numbered in the thousands to tens of thousands, gaining a sizeable region meant the rewards were significant. They could be distributed proportionally down the chain of command and keep everyone content, as well as expand and replenish forces.

But modern armies can number in the millions. And so, they can also lose soldiers in the millions to gain a relatively smaller tract of land. The result is more bloodshed, more effort expended to receive a smaller reward that has to be distributed over millions of people! Even after allowing for commanders at higher levels to get larger rewards, the final reward received per person is comparatively smaller. In other words, war gets economically unviable. In today's world, war is more localized to resource dense regions – such as oil, minerals, or bountiful soil – where efforts expended have maximum return.

It is a tremendously powerful force that can send man out to murder other humans, and to destroy towns and pillage cities. Economics (and economic incentives) are the most powerful forces in the world, as they are the chief ones capable of doing so. The other force of such power is that of hatred. Even if economic rationale behoves us to avoid war, hatred can, even under dire circumstances, continue war without end.

A rising population causes conflict in a resource strained region. A falling population may not do so if resources available are sufficient. Then, to keep war from happening, it is necessary that the human population does not rise too quickly in a region where the access to resources is uncertain.

Those Who Seek To Hurt Others Are Hurt In Of Themselves

Imagine, if one may, a sheet of glass shattered into a thousand pieces. A hand that holds a jagged piece of the glass begins to trickle blood. The harder it squeezes the piece, the deeper the piece cuts into the skin and the more readily does the blood flow.

Great Strength Can Be Found Among The Modest In Our Midst

In a populous city lived there a woman. And this woman bare a child, who, through misfortune, had crooked limbs, and a frail frame. The woman watched over her child attentively and brought him up with care. It was to little avail though, for in his twenty and first year the boy passed away. The bereaved woman spent years tormented with grief and would roam the streets weighed with sorrow. Then one day it chanced she saw a young lad who had legs splayed on either side and carried himself on the knuckles of his hands. And the lady had pity on the boy and brought him into her house. Soon, her house opened to more of the afflicted and became known in those parts. When the woman died, her work was continued by a small organization which looked after and fostered those with the short hand of fate.

This woman had not much education. She did not come from an illustrious family. She did not win any election to be Prime Minister or Premier of any state, nor could she boast conquest of any land or riches gained through trade. She was, and is, the everyman and everywoman who labour daily and earn their keep. The ones who till the lands, or thresh the grains, or resolve social issues, or protect the area. No song is written about her, no tale told of her, no one visits her grave, or remembers her kindly nature, and she herself received scant praise when she toiled while alive.

There Are No Losers

The Battle of Cannae was Rome's worst defeat, where eighty thousand Roman troops were completely annihilated. The opposing general from Carthage – Hannibal – had employed the ingenious double-envelopment strategy. During battle his troops had been able to surround the enemy heavy infantry and had hemmed them in – so much so that many soldiers could barely move. Then when his superior cavalry returned after having chased off the Romans, they attacked from the rear and caused a complete rout.

The few who escaped and returned to Rome were treated contemptuously by the populace. The Roman people thought them cowards who had run away from a major battle, and scorned and rejected these men. All, but for a man named Publius Scipio.

Scipio did not treat these men with disdain. On the contrary, he gathered together those who had fought and tried to reconstruct the events that had led to such a large defeat for the seasoned Roman army. He then trained them over time, prepared them for battle, and gave them the opportunity to fight once again against the Carthaginians, a second chance to draw swords against an old enemy.

In the intervening years, Roman strength and resilience had pushed the Carthaginians, except Hannibal, out of their territory, and Scipio was selected the commander in charge of the army to be sent across the sea – to Africa. Scipio surprisingly won battle after battle in Africa and, in desperation, the Carthaginian Senate finally recalled Hannibal back to Africa. The future of the Mediterranean World would be decided by a fight between these two generals – the one who had contested Rome in its own territory, and the other who had vowed to fight for the fatherland – at a place called Zama. This time Hannibal was fighting on African, instead of Italian soil, and against an adversary who had studied his tactics in detail.

The Battle of Zama was closely fought, and at one point, Hannibal nearly won. But Scipio rallied his men, kept the fight on, and in the end, the superior light cavalry of the Roman allies won the day. For his victory, Scipio received the epithet 'Africanus', and was greeted as a hero upon his return. Rome was now Master of the Mediterranean.

To say Hannibal's exploits were extraordinary would be to downplay any action he took. The man marched an entire army, along with war elephants, across the Alps and descended like an ancient fury upon the Italian peninsula. There, in hostile territory, he faced and consistently won battles against larger, better equipped armies led by veteran generals. At the battles of Trebia, Lake Trasimene, and Cannae, he engineered the total destruction of opposing armies, a feat unheard of then, or since. Cannae was his masterpiece, *the* archetypal battle of annihilation. To counter him, the Romans took the rare step of appointing a dictator – Quintus Fabius. Quintus Fabius finally figured the one way to deal with the intrepid general – the Fabian Doctrine – which was never to engage Hannibal directly, but to attack his allies and harass his supply lines. Despite this, and receiving no support or reinforcements from the Carthaginian Senate, through sheer singular strength he held the Roman legions at bay and threatened the Italian heartland for decades. It was only the single loss he had at Zama that made the Carthaginians lose faith in him, in his invincibility, and ended the Punic War in Rome's favour.

Man's opinion of others is mostly static and changes little once made. The same man regards himself, though, as a dynamic individual, capable of change and improvement. Few people have the ability to ascribe the same quality to others they do to themselves.

After the war, Hannibal and Scipio Africanus, as was his new appellation, ceased their individual enmity, grew to know each other and developed a mutual respect. Once when they met, Scipio asked Hannibal whom he would consider the greatest general. Hannibal replied that he would give first place to the Emperor Alexander of Macedonia, a universal choice for any general of that time. Second, he said, would be Pyrrhus of Epirus, 'for his boldness, which sets a general apart from his peers'. And third, he said, would be 'the humble personage who stands before you. For when I was young I conquered Hispania and I crossed the Alps with an army, the only man to do so since Hercules.' Scipio heard the answer, and paused a while, and seemed to contemplate his next few words. Then he proceeded ahead and asked, 'And what would you say of the general who fought the Battle of Zama?' Hannibal finally perceived what it was the general sought to know, and smiled and said, 'Had I won Zama, I would have held myself even above Alexander!'

THE PRESENT

The Present

Can principles of creation be utilized in a concrete manner rather than being an interesting theoretical digression – an unreachable abstract? What indeed would one seek when happening to wade across the hidden truths of the universe? What less but paradise, the ultimate dream, where individuals and beings have nought but delight and joy in life and their surroundings! A séance of oneness yet celebration of the individual in a passion which sustains and steadily rises in every aspect of beauty, accomplishment, and ambition!

If we delineate with clarity the most pressing of issues, they would pertain to that of poverty, of being unable to marshal sufficient resources to satisfy one's immediate needs. Can this be resolved in a manner that would evermore preclude its return? For this purpose, we turn to a basic motif that, without understanding the underlying cause of an issue, any solution would be at most a stopgap or temporary relief before it must be addressed again.

If one sifts past the veils put forth by the arrogance of modernity, poverty has always been a pox on mankind. The crux of its nature lies in the fact that no matter the resources available in a region, any inhabiting organism multiplies until the resources there become scarce. This merely keeps with the evolutionary instinct to breed copiously when there is a surplus of food. In consequence, from trees to dinosaurs to mammals, each species spread around acquiring as large a population as the land could hold. Evolution does not care how much an individual suffers, only whether he perpetuates his genes or not. And as can be observed, there are species in the hardiest of climes, from the frigid zones of the poles to the inhospitable wastes of the arid desert.

Should the problem of poverty then be considered as insurmountable, as a futile pursuit doomed to utter and abject failure? Not quite, for if we see ahead, we have two advantages in tackling the problem. One is the power of thought which allows man to probe every aspect of a problem, decide a set of actions for its resolution, and change accordingly. The other is that of technology – unavailable for the billions of years life had been before humans started to proliferate.

We can attempt a solution in a way that appears superficial on the surface, but would actually be far more powerful than first deemed. The First Principle of Creation states that we will always move toward a life of struggle. Poverty simply follows this law. But what this law does not specify is the *kind* of struggle required. Even the struggle of writing a book, or of sculpting an enviable body, is still as valid a struggle as that of coming out of poverty. Evolution is not discriminatory in this manner that one is allowed but not the other, which gives us the power to choose one over the other!

Does this differ from previous stabs taken at solving the problem? There have been attempts, since one has been able to record history, to address and perhaps find an appropriate way to handle the issue. All of them have been unsuccessful. There have always been taxes and charity given to those in need and societal programs of upliftment. None have been able to permanently affect change. The reason for that is very simple – they attempted to *remove* the struggle rather than *replace* the struggle with another. That is why they either failed or are ongoing programs. A true program successful in its objective would end, as it would end poverty itself!

To proceed, struggle can be divided into two categories – good and bad. It is quite intuitive to decide which struggle would be which. A bad struggle is that in which the individual does not have a choice due to his circumstances – for instance, going hungry or undertaking back breaking labour or being bullied. These have corresponding good counterparts – fasting to be healthier, exercise to improve the body, or light-hearted ribbing.

Can this truly be effective? If we consider the impact struggle has on our psyche, it indicates to our rather rudimentary and primitive brains, despite the recent emergence of logical thought, that the time is not yet ripe to produce offspring, that one needs settle other matters before, or that having fewer offspring would be a better option. This, coupled with technology advancements that raise the resources available for a population, can keep the human population at a reasonable margin *below* what can be supported by food sources, rather than just *at par or above*.

Note this only allows for the *procurement* of sufficient resources which may be necessary. The *distribution* of resources to the populace is a separate problem.

It is less challenging for a person with means to substitute one struggle with another. But what of the person without the capacity to do so? Here the might of technology surfaces. Specifically, specialized robots can be enlisted to provide what may be required to one who is unable to do so for himself. Farming the lands, distributing the grain, processing the foods – all can be completely automated away. After all, who would enjoy menial and repetitive labour that would be done better and more efficiently by a machine?

The Spark Of The Individual

People are, it may come as a surprising statement, generally good. The vast majority of people want to work and earn their keep. Businessmen do need employees at key roles and offer jobs at reasonable, or market, wages. Politicians try to ensure local people in the area get suitable jobs by providing appropriate incentives to companies. Unions make cases for proper wages and treatment if they seem unfair.

And yet, if one peers from above and garners an overview unfiltered by the limitations of individual bearing, one can notice a startling fact. Despite the optimal decisions taken by scrupulous and diligent people – be it worker or businessman, politician or employment agency in their varying roles, we can still reach a sub-optimal state. There exists a better state – that of robots doing it all.

It is likely we may yet reach that state despite efforts made to the contrary for which person can compete with a machine – untiring, efficient, productive, and cold-hearted! However, to the unbiased eye, this state would not only be tolerable but also preferable. After all, no one should have to work. Let the machines do it all! But to do this and simultaneously keep one's sanity, one needs have another struggle to which one can put one's mind, engage oneself and delve satisfaction from. These are the art forms that machines cannot do. Be it music or painting, writing, scientific research, or sports, these are the areas man can turn to and not only stay engaged, but derive a far greater contentment – that of a profound sexual nirvana. Man is engrossed in a fancy of his choosing which is not called work. None of the mundane tasks of delivery or production or service belong in this new world. It is a world with an unemployment rate of 100% and yet of personal advancement!

And it is a world where all needs are fulfilled at a price that is close to free. For robots do not and have never charged a penny for their labour. Nobody has paid for electricity, they have paid for the workers and investors under whose effort it has been produced. Likewise, petrol does not take any money from us for itself. It is the operation of drilling and delivery, carried out by people, that gives it a cost.

Money loses its relevance in this world, for when food and good clothes are available as is, nobody needs coin. Are we doomed, then, to a life of aimless pleasures and promptly fulfilled desires? Our currency then will be of a different kind – that of *prestige*. For just as water is essential to life, and yet no one can name those who bear us the water, the abundancc of goods does not behove us to learn about, or even appreciate, the robots that bring them about. It is rarity we are drawn to, rarity that has an impression. Ask any cricket aficionado records made in cricket and the players who achieved them, and you would get back an answer very quickly. Thence humans too shall move in this direction, striving to create a work that is lasting, and that is unique in itself. Man exerts an effort today for money; tomorrow he may yet do so, but for *prestige*.

And then there are those to whom the heart beckons. Those who are swayed not by monetary gains or personal glory. People who are more in tune with their inner instincts, and who perhaps may have a sense of fulfilment unique to themselves. There are, and have been, great artists who were not appreciated in their lifetimes, or who were popular only among a small circle of people. That these people continued with their works attests to the fact that personal drive and satisfaction are difficult to quantify. Whatever works for one is good for one, though, may not be for another.

The promised world is one where everything is free, and yet everyone fiercely indulges his own passion.

Community Spirit And The Human Mind

In the previous section we examined the nature of poverty, which has a direct physiological effect on a person. Here we look at the mental aspect of a person. Why is it that anxiety, worry, and depression are more common today? Why is it that though many have access to their heart's desire of food, or to the world's information at the touch of a screen, or on demand entertainment, we feel more lonely, more secluded, and less connected with the people around us?

Let us examine our past here, for if we surmise that something has changed for the worse compared to how it was previously, then we must explore what it is that was different then. And this isn't investigating our more recent history a few thousand years ago, nor the times human beings were before writing was developed, but the millions of years we spent as a species in the forests, on trees.

And if we were to observe this spectacle, we would notice that man spent much time in the wild with his mates. He either went hunting or foraging for supplies with the group. The ongoing exercises created a sturdy body and a dynamism with his friends, where each had a sense of what the other would do and his specific role in a particular activity. Namely, we formed communities that worked in harmony, feasted in concert, and relaxed in each other's company. Our minds have been developed to seek out, handle, and be at ease in a common circle of people.

Then we switch to a modern world, where technology has altered lives in what would be an evolutionary instant. Our behaviour was crafted by millions of years spent on trees, and now confronts abrupt changes in lifestyle in a few hundred, or at most, a few thousand years. We are not equipped to conform so quickly to such changes, and it does affect us mentally.

Progress involves having a certain protection from exposure to the elements. This consists of the building of lodgings which offer shelter from rain, wind, and the cold. As the ages advanced, more people started living in these lodgings, or houses. And then, gradually, the number of inhabitants in a dwelling began to reduce, until finally what we have is usually one family per home. Houses create a very literal barrier between those inside and the ones outside. Furthermore, in our age, usually a person gets a room for himself or himself and his spouse, which is yet another partition between the self and the other household inhabitants. Imagine that we come equipped with minds that are comfortable and actively seek out a manageable number of people to interact with – and we are left with doing so with far fewer. It is akin to using a supercomputer to perform basic arithmetic.

While it holds true that we socialize with friends and colleagues, the notion of the house is baked in as a spot separate from our external jaunts. Our thoughts and talk are of a different kind within the household as compared to without, and they may further differ within the confines of one's room. The reason for these are the very concrete walls that, to a rational mind, should be opaque in actuality and transparent in effectiveness. Our minds, though, are primitive, and logic and reason are relatively new concepts not ingrained in us beyond a surface layer. While we establish relationships with others, it is less effective than knowing each other by staying together.

An argument can be made that man should not be dependent on external factors to have balance. There are masters who have detached themselves from worldly necessities and proceeded to enrich the world. We too can disavow positive deep relationships with each other and live a life of rigor but there is no need to do so. It is something that was joyous and routine and can continue to be so!

The solution to the housing issue is simple – tear down all walls! Be, or emulate the open prairie living enjoyed, despite then having continual threats to survival, by our ancestors. A community that thrives on the rich interpersonal relations among its members.

Removing walls and having people be beside each other is a precondition, but it is the activities that are done together that create the community spirit. Otherwise, we would be left by something similar to a mall, where people are around, but ignore each other in their wanderings to obtain material goods. For another kind of wall it is that separates each from the other – that of the ego; that of having, or pursuing personal desires and being content within one's space of acquisitions and acquaintances. It doesn't harm one to smile at a fellow being sometime!

One must mention, before bringing to a close the chapter, that rooms do provide a solitude that is useful primarily for reflection, introspection, and unconventional outpourings of thought. Many great mathematicians and writers have had to themselves nought but a room and some scraps of paper. We do have the outdoor equivalent of this as well, where a single person could go off by himself into the woods or beside a river to get inspiration.

All Creations Provide A Window Into The Soul Of The Creator

We live in privileged times. The best of all pieces of music, of literature, of scientific research are available more conveniently and expeditiously than the time it takes to get groceries. Just as walls create a psychological barrier between us, books link our minds with their creators. Once more, we see the fallibility of the human mind, in that though it knows the author is not physically present, it presumes some form of him being there. In contrast to what was previously a separating influence, artistic works serve as a bonding experience. A creator pours his soul into his work, and one who peruses it converses and garners an insight into his soul.

The artist leaves behind an impression of his soul even after he is dead. If we hear the pieces of Beethoven, we can feel the angst and immense agonies he went through as he suffered to write music he himself could never hear, for he was deaf. Access to the works of these great men and women allows us to form 'phantom communities' where one can interact with them, but alas, in a unidirectional way.

Gardens Are A Luxury Today Whereas They Were Commonplace In The Ancient World

Though the change has happened slowly, urban lives are spent roaming, staying, and resting in stone quarries (or buildings)! Even perchance were we to venture outside, what we would see are layers upon layers of concrete separated by tar hardened roads. Only at specific times, when we consciously choose so, we head to a garden and are at ease among the trees and the shrubbery.

Natural locations – as gardens, forests, meadows, beaches, mountains, rivers, lakes, and valleys – secretly and inconspicuously allow the best of our ethos to be wrought – and in a relaxed way; for these are where all creatures have had comfortable habitats since before they became self-aware. In our technological haste, in the infernal race to increase materialistic products and to acquire lavish quarters, we have lost that which was most comforting, most calming, most joyous, and most conducive to inspiring oneself!

The complete removal of urban lifestyle may be futuristic, but at present much of a natural landscape can be integrated with existing environment. Consider buildings without walls, whose floors are covered in grass, where plants and trees peek out of carved holes, and ponds and streams of water flow in our midst!

The Hunter Gatherer Diet

It is human tendency to distil from very complex phenomena core ideas, inscribed in key words or symbols, which, upon sufficient application of pre-ordained rules, yield and explain their mysteries. Mathematics uses axioms and logical steps to derive astounding relationships among an infinitude of numbers. Physics can, using a few equations, describe the future pathways a system under study may undergo.

Yet one must be wary of dismantling intricate structures and stuffing their presumed components into cubby holes. As one moves away from the purer sciences, from mathematics to physics to chemistry and further, complexity may be an intrinsic part, unable to be expressed in a few impressionable syllables.

Modern diet is a sample case. A few decades back, experts said it was fat in our diet that caused health issues to humans. Then, as research progressed, they began to say there are good fats and bad fats, and we still need good fats for our upkeep. Today, sugar is considered a prime source of many ailments like obesity, diabetes, ageing, and heart problems. But the truth is – if one ingests the same sugar by eating natural foodstuffs like sugarcane or bananas, none of these problems appear! And research has begun to admit as much.

What then are we lacking in our studies? For there is little doubt that the research is not done conscientiously with due attention to various parameters involved. The peer review process also rigorously verifies the claims made. The mistake lies in the postulate that certain nameable nutrients, like fats or sugar or carbohydrates or vitamin Bs or beta carotenes or minerals, which were in excess amount or deficient in the study, were the cause. For every nutrient we can identify and measure, there are thousands of similar or dissimilar unnamed ones that are present in a certain proportionality and contribute to the overall results.

The reason? Our bodies have developed over millennia eating organic foods, not just vitamins or minerals or proteins. As apes in the wilderness, we ate fruits, vegetables, nuts, seeds, and grains and our bodies are accustomed to absorb nutrients that are part of the *holistic whole*. Internal to the cell, thousands of proteins interact in millions of pathways to keep it functional. But understanding a few mechanisms and a couple of nutrients that enhance them does not provide a comprehensive insight into its biology. Other nutrients may be needed, in smaller proportions, to achieve our optimal goals. This is why supplements, while an innovative concept, may not be as effective as eating their corresponding organic foods. One can prefer spinach to taking vitamin B pills.

Our prehistoric bodies are unsure how to handle processed foods, such as potato chips, soft drinks, chocolates, and pies. For these are foods that never were available before the 20th century. Thence these are the chief ones that may cause health issues, obesity and other problems. It is not the cholesterol, calories, or carbohydrates in them that are responsible for health problems. They are simply foods we have not been evolutionarily programmed to assimilate.

If there is a word to choose, be that our innate need, it would be *organic.* We may never understand in its fullness, its richness, and in its grandiose majesty, the glorious process of digestion.

Can Existing Communities Be Improved Upon?

That communities are formed is inevitable. That they have existed since the lines were blurred between ape and man is indisputable. That they may be gently nudged to become even more potent is a distinct – and enticing – possibility.

There are two aspects one can consider when one probes various communities – inter community relations and the ability of a community to have its members gain significant abilities they could not have done so without. The first of these used to be based on how the leaders of each community interacted. For, as it is difficult for all members in one community to meet and have a rapport with all of another, it used to suffice that selected representatives from either would do so.

Or is it? Can we perhaps derive a mechanism by which individual members can yet form connections? Let us explore a method that does that.

Choose three from within one community to partake in the exercises of another. Why three? One person would simply become a member of the other community and two as the smallest group possible would not provide enough diversification of thought. If three, possibly different, members could be represented in a different community five days a week, that itself would link the community to five other communities.

The above technique has been tried in some way before, but not methodically and with definite intent. What gives this way more power is the *exponential* increase in the links with different communities if every community starts to follow this. Beyond first-degree connections, at the fourth or fifth level, we would have a single community linked with almost any other community chosen at random – and at the base level!

And these links are stronger, because multiple members are involved. They can cause better techniques and innovations to be incorporated more quickly past a longer chain of intermediary communities. Relatively unrelated disciplines can influence findings and developments in others via cross-pollination of ideas. Music in some faraway land may influence the creation of a game in another!

Furthermore, in olden times, the relationship between communities was dependent more on the personalities of their leaders. If there was friction between two leaders, it percolated down to their groups. When communities are linked together at the ground level, the caprices of their leaders can be mostly ignored. For leaders are nought but an agglomeration of the general thoughts and feelings of the community.

No King Ever Held
A Smartphone In His Hand

Pharaohs, kings, emperors, rajahs, shehenshahs and their ilk were at times regarded as gods or deities in their own realms and worshipped in adulation. All the power and knowledge attributed to them of a god, though, was not enough to have a single one of them make an electronic gadget, or hold one.

How do we know today is verifiably different over what was a hundred or a few thousand years ago? What particular metric do we pick to demonstrate that progress has been made from a previous age? For every age has had aspects to its culture that are similar today, with few modifications. Politics, governments, religion, business, art, charity, trade, travel have all existed since antiquity, all with similar structures, promises, and designs.

The difference is that today business can be conducted on a smartphone and political promises of a utopian society are streamed online.

As when somebody sees a palace in a lake, and leaps into it, only for the palace to disappear in ripples, so it is with much touted among the masses. Technology is the true mark – the veneer that exhibits the extent of man's achievement. And creative works as well: for today we have the paintings of Dali, of Picasso, and the incomparable music of Tchaikovsky, Beethoven, and Mozart. Which king in a previous age could boast of listening to such music, or having a collection of such artwork?

As Beethoven once said, 'Prince, what you are, you are through chance and birth; what I am, I am through my own labour. There are many princes and there will continue to be thousands more, but there will only be one Beethoven.'

And finally, isn't improvement in community a simple consequence of the artistic pursuit of the individual. Stripped of all pretence and show, it is a carnal instinct. To bring into being something new, something different, something radical, an act or deed or creation daring, special, and extraordinary, which would not exist were it not for the creator and which the world would not be fortunate to behold otherwise.

THE FUTURE – INTO THE REALM OF THE MYSTICAL

The Painting

'Twas in the past, and the future, was there a man and a woman in a house. And the man was possessed of a sexual vigor manic and enviable, crazed and reserved. Pleasures of the flesh the couple had, loud and whispered, controlled and uncontrollable, dark and resplendent. Such cries and riotous thumps issued from the abode, immodest and immoderate in their excess. Questions arose, natural and deliberate, but still obvious and prolific, and their concision could be compressed into one word – why?

Nobody knew. Nobody understood. No couple had the kind of relentless unwavering capability and unspeakable exogenous delights. It was not meet, nor ceremonial, not found nor given. And the man himself posed this legitimacy and carried its bulk until he was required of a resolution.

And the man began to pray to the gods, fervently, incessantly, for he was of a tenacious and firm authority. They were not different from everyone otherwise, but for a single discrepancy, and he sought the reason for it. The woman understood not his keenness and desire for reason, but he could neither be cajoled nor persuaded; and so she turned from the topic. There he may have remained, steadfast and pugilistic, praying and meditating still with a devout fervour had it not been for a god to appear before him one day.

Who he was, remains undetermined, and inconclusive. He was tall, taller than a house and tall enough to halt the foreboding winds that blew above. He was garnished of a substance not of earth; it blazed lightly, and its hue was tangential, and effusive, and no eye could penetrate it. He spoke though, and he spake with a deep and evocative tone, much as when the sea parts its waves.

'Halt your austerities, man of concern. The gods be well pleased with you! Lay your position before the might of our splendour!' And the man looked up, unafraid, but still of a disbelief, and made query as to who the apparition was.

'I am sent of the gods. That you may know you have been heard, and will be treated of a receipt agreeable, and fateful. I am Corazin, the God of Reassurance. Put forth the turbulent streams that beset you in!'

The man, seated yet on a small mound, and unclothed but for a loincloth, stated, 'I thought not my meditations bear this fruit, that I be before the power and stately esteem of a god. Verily it is, they say, the discovery of penance guides one to uncommon bounties. I be well, not because I may obtain at last that for which I strove, but that I tasted, and harboured close, the harsh plainness and yet unimaginable exult of my penance.

'My effort, intense in focus, and of an incredible endurance, generated much heat, depth, and energy. That is contained within me, but needs be released. And when it does so, I fear the power therein set free, to surround, envelop tight, and squeeze and consume the very universe, and every being in it. For this be the pure emanation of *tapas*, the highest, and most concentrated, spiritual fire.

'Thence I ask of ye, as asked it is of me – to take safe from me this power that may violate the normal course of the living, and render void this threat that it pass unnoticed.'

'Aha!' said the apparition. 'Much power is built up in you – one can see from the radiance that comes off your chest. Your concern be our concern too, for we do not wish the world be needlessly put to an end. How then would we watch, and draw satisfaction, on what unfolds as time moves on?

'Time, then, be the answer to your question. It be of a fact, were you to release the energy held within you, it would destroy the universe. But if you gave shape to your power, and gained control over it, you could diffuse it slowly throughout the universe at every time instant, from the beginning of time to the end. Doing so, the power would dissipate – and that without harm. For at each instant, a tiny fraction of the power would spread across the universe, and seep into it without damage.'

The man heard this and, the argument being sensible, attempted the same, and was pleased to note a level of competence within himself – he could manipulate and bring shape to the inestimable power in him. Thence he moved once more into the realm of trance – the esoteric, placid spot that teemed and brimmed with potential, and there he drew clear the line – he knew not, and could explain not, how – but of a conviction that he could slowly release his power along it, exactly as was described by the god. And as the power ebbed, he sensed it was contained – welcomed even – by that which was, which is, and which is to be. And he expressed relief, and gratitude for the assistance received.

'It be but essential and necessary,' dismissed the god amid a friendly wave. 'And I be responsible for none of it, for it is you who set the manner of execution, you who attempted it, and you who fulfilled it. None shall be aware of it and that too is as it is to be.

'Thereby, that this be not regarded so, ask ye again what boon it is you seek. Beware though, and ask what lies in the depths of your heart, for you will not be given another chance!'

And the man then bare the absolute of his need, a sombre yet uncanny desire and he rent its tangled condition and offered its primal pieces before the site of the risen.

The god stood visibly disconcerted, and he prowled the grass on light feet, hither and thither, afore he submitted to the comfort of a seat atop a copse of trees. There he gazed – bemused and nonplussed – and his rendition finally vacated the nub of all expressions:

'But people usually request for that substantial gift which affords them betterment in their voluptuous practices! Never have I been presented such a plea, ludicrous in all it entails, and from one who already has that which other people direct their lust upon! Why do you wish to extricate the reason behind your coital relishes!?'

And the god wrung his hands furiously, and settled his jaw upon them, and turned taciturn. The silence in the arena swelled, and spread, and was pertinent. An appropriate amount of time went by, as it should, until the awkwardness of the situation was assuredly flagrant.

'So!' said the god, 'I see from your demeanour and your lack of inclination to further expression that your demand be well and true. But I must say, it be not for me to turn true the reckon, that ye be content and whole. Not that I be unable, or unwilling, but my powers be restrained and they be for physical alteration not to compose those refined sentences whose utterance curbs your curious impulses. I offer ye this counsel though, to rectify, and submit, that the higher power be yet of a relevance.

'To the west, and north of these lands, go. And as you travel past valleys, and forests, and streams, ask ye around for the Forgotten Mountain. There it is stays still a great master. He it is who has acquired of a penchant to gather unlikely patterns and he knows of those arguments freed of the tempest of time. He be the one to relieve you of your venturesome want.'

Thusly he spake, and he swivelled, and huffed, and hurried off, little burdened and overly exaggerated.

As the sun came down upon the house, its inhabitants were astir with excitement, and wonderment. Several plans had been discussed, considered, adopted, and discarded. The woman was most affected by the frenzy and her face stayed flush and warm in preparatory anticipation. As their energies lay unabated, she bustled around the place, rummaging, choosing, pausing, and returning. Eventually her ministrations began to be directed to the other occupant of the house, and she came close, and felt the roughened exterior, and sported a lascivious smile. And she dragged of his person into the personal room. And she polished her knees on the bedroom nightstand.

In the morning by the lush grass bed beside the stream, the couple started off on a journey they supposed to be long and searching. Passed they different areas of changing landscapes and did survey from the locals as to the path. And they were encouraged by the quizzical faces and ignorance professed by those spoken to. For did that not mean they were on the right path, just far away from where they had to be?

Much can be spoken of, and written, about their traipse through the plains. Through forests and hills, river valleys and meadows, gorges and ravines, at each spot they encountered contrasted and surprising beings. Suffice to put it, as they sped on, the general tone of the voices grew from that unsure to those doubtful to faint remembrance to quiet dispersal to undiluted fear. That gave them hope, for they followed the fear and doggedly went where the fear increased until the lands were sparse of both habitants and vegetation. Some discreet force kept away life forms from that place. It had been whispered to them in manifold ways – 'Those who go there return not, and are subject to an impartial law!' 'The powers there reduce the senses of a man until he becomes but a shrivelled and hollowed case subsumed by malevolent entities!'

But despite the warnings, they reached finally the shores of the sea, whose beaches were utterly barren and desolate – a pink desolation, but for assorted huts, pockmarked ice, dreary slabs, and worn down boats. It had evidently been abandoned for much time. Not a living organism was to be found – in the huts, or on the beach, or even in the boats, or beneath the ice pickings. Not crabs, fish, seaweed, or algae. Bereft of life, in that moist cold that clutched at the inner organs, they rested on pink sand, despondent and exhausted. As night approached, no sound could be felt. Not an owl hooted or cricket chirped. A strangely quiet night draped a pitch black cover over the silent beach, for though the waves rolled to and fro, they could not be heard.

They picked a larger hut and huddled close. The lone blanket did not dispel the cold entirely. In that chill, somehow their bodies warmed each other, a slight exchange, but still, that little glimmer that leads to the dangling temptation of hope. And amid a withdrawing but still tense occlusion, a fiery spirit awoke, which had been unknowingly dormant, and the drive of the masculine was consummated by the acquisition of the receptive feminine. In an incident taken note of by none, the silence of the dark night was punctuated by soft cries, moans, grunts, high pitched shrieks, and relentless pronounced screams, perhaps a first seen since its desertion.

Then as dawn rose, in an escapade of much courage, gall, and foolishness, they took the refuge of a larger vessel, and in it set sail in a direction away from the lands and toward the unknown. For the small yet significant hold of trial espoused the innate quality of a slightly reckless seeking, that facilitated an astute ignorance, and yet carefree pursuit.

How long they were at sea – none know, as is the requirement. Several times they almost washed out, and several times the sea drew them back into its loving deadly bosom. Of hunger, or thirst, or thought, they lost all sense, and had no bearing as to their path. Eventually worked they, their hands, and their wrists, on pure but formidable instinct. And in that haze, that battered and clammy state that tugged and wrestled impolitely, did they descry finally the shores of a new land. And they leaped into the water, and waded ashore, all drenched and doused in a sweltering rain. And they did reach true, o my friends, upon the slopes of the large mountain. Pink in colour, akin to the sands of the far away opposing beach, and a crest that jutted proudly into the sky, it stood unopposed and evident, serene and nonchalant. The crystal peak and sooth aroma welcomed the exhausted pair and caressed tenderly their vulnerable frames. And for as long as their bodies recalled, they hugged the surface and slept, too tired to examine their surroundings.

The Mountain

It was a strange mountain, not in the normal way strangeness is assessed; for it was a mountain like all others, albeit pink. There were paths that led upward, though no human life had settled the place. As the couple explored further, they found plants and trees aplenty, which was well, for they could eat, be fed, and sleep peaceably. Only when they approached the higher regions, they saw animals, or mobile life forms.

The search was a queer and curious one, for though they tried, their attempts were futile, and they had only the company of goats. No other animals walked the winding and uneven pathways. They did not see cows, oxen, horses, or dogs, much less humans, though different kinds of birds roosted in the area as well.

One feature about the mountain that puzzled them further was – only the half of it that faced them was accessible. If one tried to go to the edge, or try and go around, the slopes of the mountain became sheer walls, unclimbable and untraversable. The other side of the mountain was inaccessible – a mysterious enigma.

Let us return again to our traveling companion, the man whose perseverance had deposited him on the insensate location. His sojourn had been hard and our captain was now an afflicted man. His walk and gait were stern, his face dreamy, and he kept extending his hand, were he to ward off an invisible malignancy.

The lack of variety in the animals was a conundrum exceeded only by the observance of the man speaking to a goat one day. The woman besought his reason for the act, but the man merely warded her off and asserted it was because it had to be. This caused friction 'tween the two, and the woman went off and was by her own for a while. In the evening, the man met her by the cliffside, and she relented, and was responsive to his advances, and did not mention their earlier discord. They clasped palms, and he rubbed her sides teasingly and she swayed her hips vivaciously, and rested her head on his chest, and smote his ribs playfully with her hand. He was gratified she had mollified, and their gentle touches turned rougher, as did the intensity of their passion. Her lush red lips brushed, and felt the upper shoulder and neck. Below heaved the stimulating concern of luxurious breasts, a generous bosom the swell and rise of whose fecundity invited welcomingly. Warm blood suffused her face and it acquired a fresh richness. Beautiful eyes looked up and laughed coaxing. Within the enclosed drapery of loose garment, her body was ripe, fragrant, exuded heat, and the woman swivelled to the inclination of an elegant and fruitful posterior. The man finally loosened his tongue and a stream of syllables escaped his expanded lungs. A chivalric yet ferocious desire growled his pent up charge, the inferno from the pits of his loins.

And on that overhanging cliff that gazed down upon the scenic mellow coast, before the dubious calls and squawks of the cormorants and the blue finches, the swallows and the seagulls, he expended the surge of his libido to the rush and flushed exuberance that simmered with urgency and turbulence. The seminal surge rose always getting nearer, and closer, until the loss of all restraint led to the unstopping exertion of profligacy that drove the reserves past withdrawal potential.

The pods burst. The compressed energy exploded. A primal preliminary shock suddenly thrust through from the root past the edges to the exposed tip before the containment was opened and vital stores released. Involuntary, unstoppable spasms squeezed gathered content into travelling tubes whose winding palpable path diverged appropriately before the flow was directed into a single extension. The perpendicular shaft quivered with conduction and anticipation. The latent elongation erupted, and in the confines spewed a liberal issuance of copious virile fluid in intermittent spurts and eviscerating ejections. Gradually, the streams became lesser and smaller until every ounce of desire had been expunged. Though emptied and retracted, the priapic member still continued small pleasurable throbs, a token to the dynamic release of the previous moment, while the receptacles relaxed, content having expelled the abundance.

What followed was a reminder of relief that came from the primary masculine organ at its emptiness while the immediate faculties moved into a sedate peacefulness.

Unfortunately, once a man begins to parley with goats, the habit is not one rid of easily. However, the matter turned out to be of some concern when it was discovered he had turned into one himself.

Not much could be done. The transformation took but a few seconds, appeared painless and natural, and was disturbed by the abundant shrieks of a female that pierced incongruously the wholesome atmosphere. She had been collecting wood and had returned to witness the incident.

She was by a tree, and leaned her bulk against it, and sobbed, her tender fingers grazing the wood. But being of a sturdy mind, she steadied, and began to edge to the spot, intent and cautious. She came by the side of the goat when another brisk event occurred that disconcerted her, befuddled her, and had her heaped on the ground.

The goat's body expanded in every direction, openly, egregiously, plaintively, and assumed once more a human frame. He was there before her again – the same man – full of flesh and manly characteristics.

She rushed to the spectre and her behaviour indicated a multitude of reactions – she was simultaneously angry, afraid, bewildered, confused, and worried, and his undue laughter did not help proceedings.

It took a while, but after some impassioned explanations, her excessive but reasonable queries were quenched. The conversation was long, interrupted, and probed different aspects, but the gist was – the man had learned, somehow, eerily, to metamorphose into an animal at will. The details are hazy, and of a great secret, for it cannot, and should not, be revealed to just anyone. And it was disbelieved by the living soul beside him too, until she tried the technique herself. And she was astonied at having the body of a goat, the bleat of a goat, and the shaggy beard of a goat!

As with any creature that gains a modicum of prowess, and casts about to perceive its furthest reaches, the ability to alter at will their physical structure inveigled our curious couple to change form, and feel, and probe from within, species of varying sizes, and shapes. And the mountainside was littered over time with the visual sights of animals from ants to spiders, fleas to eagles, dogs to elephants, a reprieve from the usual depiction of goats.

It stands to reason then, that two animals of the same kind would execute the one recreation available them while traversing a faraway place of much intrigue.

And as is, conjugal experiences myriad began with thrilling novelty, and escalated to a frenzied turbulence, from which emanated a daunting mix, that graduated to a hopeful emergence and finally subsided into tranquil resolution.

But before we address the meat of the affair – the inevitable denouement – the assumption of skins and minds of fauna allowed views into the world unlike that of humans. Through cockroaches, they saw the world as a mosaic of dots, black and white. When dogs, they sensed fragrances and the aura of various natural elements from afar too. As eagles they soared into the sky with sharp penetrating eyes and espied verily the smallest fern below, and they twisted, and wheeled, and performed acrobatics while aloft to immense pleasure and thrill. And they realized the variety in outlook of the world held in reserve yet a quiet unity – immortal but base needs. Each animal instinctively sought but sustenance and procreation. And the diversity in the senses of species was created by the same!

Despite gaining access to extra sensory faculties, they realized they could not circumvent the base rule of the location. The other side of the mountain was still forbidden to them. If they tried to burrow through as worms or rodents, they would hit a wall they could not ingest. If they attempted to fly around, the plumes of air that billowed would join in and harden and they would be left pecking futilely at it, unable to see past either.

The denouement. As tradition dictates, verbal communication of experiences – concupiscent and culinary – led to a common acknowledgment. On the matter of libidinous tendencies, both were in concord and attested as to the order of their satisfaction.

The third best format of copulation is of dolphins. Like lilting seductive flows of the sea, the marine animals glide and swerve and perform in a smooth dance, and an enchanted rhythm, and with the tinkle, rush and echo of the surrounding water, they draw closer and move apart in waves of uneven amplitudes, pendulant, touching then, withdrawing again, with light calls, until all that is observed is a harmonious arrangement, motile, but still; and when they retract eventually, no trace or assumption remains of any sort of engagement. No realization, or awareness, of the fertile activity.

Second place is occupied by pigs. Pigs neither ignore nor gloss over the happenstance. As is their nature – that of animals that trample around in the muck and the filth – pigs acknowledge the smuttiness of the act. They assume it and embrace it, they root about in the mud, rolling around with grunts, squeals and spasmodic shrieks as they climax unto orgasm.

And as may be expected, the one that is breathtaking and magniloquent, outrageous and commensurate is relegated to the homo sapiens. Its consequence is a factor of the sheer breadth and range of emotions, and positions, available, and the numerous ways affection can be encountered – beautiful, charming, vulnerable, naughty, tender, discreet, gentle, rough, quick, smooth, hard, furtive, open, oscillatory.

A common agreement was also come to regarding the difference in equilibrium among the sexes. 'Men want it more. Women enjoy it more.' Both attested to the assertion, and appreciated the renewed amity promulgated by the consensus. The male follows a prominent protuberance that seeks a corresponding inversion. Once in, though, it is the female that harbours the bulk of the agreeability. The ecstasy of the woman is ninefold when compared with the effort of the thrusting man.

And as the story unfolds we hear snippets of the conversation of the man with the goats. The talks are not, and do not seem, entirely explanatory, but we provide an exposition here nonetheless.

'You were too weak and dependent on the evil words and designs of the counsellor! Your realm was fruitful when it came to you, and you have made of it a famine, and ordered immoral wars of a diabolic nature, which you lost justly. Then when men with weapons were sent to ask of you your account, you foreswore and laid it on the counsel! You were craven, and weak – and a suitable treatment awaits you!'

And while treading a thin path he pointed at another goat – 'What did you need more that you committed such sins? Of wealth, of land, of servants, you had plenty, enough for you, enough for seven generations after you. Your king was reasonable and kindly and gave fairly based on the value each brought. And yet you, and your coterie, plotted and perforated his sides with the impolite implement! You left a good man's blood stained by his breakfast table. Is there any part of the world lowly enough to accept you? Even now, it is being chosen for you! And I would mourn that land that will be weighed down underneath you!'

And to his surprise, while he uttered these phrases the lady was silent and did not question his mutterings. He decided, after some hesitation, to uncover the burden within and he confided to her and confessed that he had had revelations.

'It is not of something new, something different that I somehow obtained, but what I always was – and am. A cotton patch is being removed not just from before my eyes, but from within my brain and I am become whole once again. I am beginning to remember.'

'You know of the past? Of people and cultures that lived before?'

'No,' said he, 'I am remembering the future.'

And there he was slightly surprised for she neither sneered nor mocked, and she regarded him not with pity or concern, but then as he garnered the reach of their tale, he had the explanation. They had landed and were installed in a strange place, and been exposed to paranormal occurrences, and their belief in the fantastic had been strengthened. They were unlike usual men and women who had to strain to believe. Thereby he continued the disclosure.

'I am aware the words I say sound fictitious, and illogical. Until now, I have but myself had to gather and correct the slow liberation of my knowledge. But of this I am sure – that the memories I am able to retrieve are those of the future!'

'Isn't the future yet to happen? And weren't we taught there can be many futures due to the differing decisions taken by people in the present?'

'There are many futures. And there are many pasts. The future and the past are in symmetry and through an unbiased lens – have no distinguishing property. Just as the present branches into multiple futures, the present is reached at by many branches from the past.'

'But everyone remembers one past and we all agree on it,' she exclaimed.

'We all agree on the gist of it. A king lived here, a king died there. A war took place in some land, a miracle happened someplace else. But no one knows the finer details. Which individual soldier fought in each war? What meal did they take on the third day of the fight?

'Just so, everyone can predict the future. It is the level of detail that decides the accuracy of the prediction. For instance, I can say a couple of hundred years from now everyone alive today will be dead. Or that the Lisith kingdom will produce a certain amount of iron and steel this year. But that is something anyone can do. What I am starting to remember of the future is as when someone remembers the past. The important events. The ones that are passed down each generation.

'The past and the future have multiple branches that combine into and emerge from the present.

'The present is all there is.

'And yet, in every branch occur the same important events.

'In our minds, when we remember an event, that is the present. These events are simply a projection of the present into the past, and the future.'

Though she understood little at first, she did comprehend it over time. But she had also noted the steady rise in his unevenness, and his tempestuousness, and she suspected rightly what was the cause.

'I am agitated,' he conceded. 'We are yet to find the master and there looks to be no trace of humans on this mountain. Sometimes I wonder if we came to the right place, but then I recall the queer path we followed and conclude – this could be the only place.' And she agreed.

Herbs, Greens, And Spices

They picked at the mountainside in the form of herbivorous animals and their enhanced perceptions drew them to reckon the varieties of herbs and plants there. Several of them they had ingested and by their smell, could predict an inherent esoteric quality in them. The herbs had unusual properties and had influenced the otherworldly tendencies in our companions. They withdrew quickly, however, from a herb that had an especially pungent smell. It was darkish green in colour and had reddish spots on the edge. The morning dew rang as light drops on it and was nearly frozen. They knew it instinctively to be the most potent of the excessively potent herbs there. To have it would be to walk the fine wire that separated life and death.

Once content after a meal of oats and hay, the couple neighed pleasantly atop a narrow pass. Hormones secreted and proliferated across sturdy torsos and soon, the stallion was erect and the mare bared the exposure of her inviting rear. And the stallion mounted of the mare to a rousing clamour. And the mare clasped the entirety of the proffered extrusion and clenched around it with a dainty hollow. There was much bellowing and snorting and delighted whinnying and the enormous tumults shifted the earth beneath them. They knew not which herb enabled it, but they were able to change form to Solemnyr – the ancient race of the king of horses, that were larger than elephants and faster than cheetahs and were supposed to have been ridden by the gods into battle against the demons. But the soil underneath could not sustain, and they fell, creating much ruckus and that would have been the end of the story, had they not come to a sudden halt. Part of the mountain jutted out and was stable enough to hold them.

They steadied and were about to laugh it off as one of the perils of unsafe conjugation, but their heightened senses caught the vagrant waft of stuffy air and had them curious. They followed the smell until a crevice in the wall was revealed to them. With some energetic smashes, the crevice widened, and they entered the orifice.

A dark passageway ran up, then down, and then straight until a large cavern opened before them. The domed cave, as it was, was fusty, musty, and dusty. It glowed lightly, for though no gaps were seen, sunlight somehow streamed through. At the centre of the cavern was a pool and to the sides were vines that intertwined and went up. The cavern was dotted with rock mounds of varying height. Across the pool was a rock mound much like a pillar, for it was squarish though the top was oblique. As they explored the cavern with trepidation, once more human, the light finally picked a prone form beside the pool.

It was a human skeleton.

Whoever he was, was dead. Most certainly. Definitely. Verifiably. And had been for a long time. Here was evidence, incontrovertible, firm, and absolute, though, that the mountainside did host life forms other than goats.

The fact did not cheer either of them.

The Black Widow

The talks the man had with the goats had begun to be slightly irritable. His face was cloudy, dark, and his thoughts convoluted.

They had spoken of leaving. He was amenable to the idea, but, surprisingly, the woman was adamant and stubbornly insisted they continue their quest. That they had found a human body, she explained, was proof they were moving ahead.

His dejection sourced from the belief the skeleton they had stumbled upon was that of the master promised; and without the master, no explanation could assuage his thirsting heart. Their trek across the plains, the journey past the oceans, and the exploration of the untimed mountain were significant accomplishments gone awry without the seal of success – a marathon run without passing the finish line.

'Your crimes were unnecessary and exorbitant!' said he to a rather young and hapless goat. 'You were to be a carpenter as your father, but you had not the patience or the ethic. Then bad men enticed you into their fold and had you murder high ranking men on the orders of a prince. Once one of them was caught though, he revealed you to be an accomplice and then neither those men nor the prince saved you from the chop!

'Had you but that foremost of qualities – discipline – not the most powerful of men could have distracted you from your occupation, and into one of disgrace and intrigue! A carpenter's job – may be unglamorous and yet, is essential, and upstanding. Be who you are, of a stern routine, and the most surprising of rewards, and positions would come to you. But you chose to intermingle with unsavoury associates and forfeited your youth!'

One day it chanced they were by a girdle of trees, and he suddenly reached for and wielded a thin stick. And he brandished of the piece and struck hard the back of a nearby goat. The goat bleated piteously and made to flee, and the man rushed after it hither and thither, flicked his arm repeatedly and whipped and dealt severely with the animal until the woman intervened and belaboured him to cease the harsh outpour of energy.

What the animal's deed was, he said not, for he recoiled from the matter, repulsed, and from his inane grunts only a few words were comprehensible such as – reprehensible, and abomination. He did mention later though that the creature had been party to 'the most gruesome and abhorrent betrayal', and that his treatment of it was justified a hundred times over, and he wished only to have been given more time to 'exact retribution'.

But the woman's thirst was piqued, and innate sensibility pricked and she demanded whether evil doings had sufficient redressal, for seemed it to her that mere representation in the nature of goats did not relegate them to an adequate reprisal.

'It is but meet!' said the man excitedly. 'Do you not see that this is the most terrible part of their punishment! That they have full knowledge of the wrongdoings they are going to commit and to be powerless to stop it! They cast out desperately into the future, yearn and urge their future selves to be different, to choose a better path, only for it to never happen. And certainly yes, oh yes, they have understanding of the appropriate punishment that awaits them later too. Each one of them would pull forward his respective punishment if he could, to undergo, and be done with, but none are allowed to do so! For anticipation of punishment is worse than punishment itself!'

However it became evident soon that the man was troubled. He continually smoothed his shaven chin and thin creases would appear unduly on his forehead. He had a perturbed mind. There was something, he knew, he needed to consider – something vital and integral – but it slipped from him sneakily when he felt he had a grasp on it. And so, almost swimmingly, he continued the dizzy plod until one day, once more, he bore his vehemence upon another ill-fated victim.

'You were the most senior minister and in your greed and your impatience to seize the throne you slew the erstwhile king! The kingdom did come to you, but you were ousted in some months. And as cannot be kept hidden, your malicious deed was laid open before the people and then what awaited you was hot roiling oil eager to swallow you in!

'Every position has its place and its utility to the permanence. Not only the ones in sight of public admiration. It isn't wrong to desire them but were you to put aside your desire and maintain the discipline of your post, you would not have to ask or seek anything, it would come to you of itself! As each part of the body performs its own task, every person in an organization has a defined role. It is discipline that has the organization thrive, and each member.

'One can hold his own role and focus and have yet ambition, goals and dreams. But to grab and yank forth an undeserved spot for oneself – neither keeps with the natural flow of state nor the esteem of every discipline. It is one who adheres to discipline who gradually flows into his desired place.'

And having thusly dispensed the required reprimand, our man walked by, a sanctimonious saunter, until a sudden and instant alignment of thoughts halted the issuance of movement signals to every muscle fibre in his body.

He paused. He trembled. He shook. Unbidden shoots struck, left, and returned until they were vivid. That which he had been searching for in earnest – the elusive sequence of statements that brought relief to a perturbed mind – had formed in him of a frightening abruptness. Gentle pearly white drops pronounced his cheeks, and the absolute of barbaric remonstrance smote him to the ground. And he stayed there, elaborately overcome and intensely anguished.

Later that day, in a manner decidedly less than serene, he made a baleful request of his feminine accomplice that was the recipient of stringent opposition. The ensuing conversation was long and contentious and to record in a modest tome, difficult. Thereby we present snippets of it.

Unfortunately it seems the man lacked a convincing reason for his extraordinary plea. He simply uttered the phrase – 'It is what must be,' and repeatedly stated the term 'force majeure'. And the other conviction he betrayed with a pale expression of regret – 'my faults led me unhesitating to the inescapable trial required. For verily I declared views, unasked and unbidden, and did acts unbecoming a humble seeker, even though they consisted of a righteous source. It was not for me to pass down justification and correction. For are there not sacred and eternal laws? And that I did so, I must face my test with tranquil resignation.'

'You ask for danger, love,' she said. 'And if I agree and were you not to survive, would your moral sense permit that I be left, all alone and bereft of my companion?'

'It is no easy thing I ask,' admitted the man. 'Not of ye, nor of me. But it must be done, not for myself, nor others – no, it is no selfish reason that I ask for it – but the inexorable laws of this world demand it be done. It is the divine mandate that decrees. Were we to interfere or attempt to change the essential course it would only postpone the inevitable and make it even harder when eventually it bears down upon us.

'If I fail, and that be quite possible, I assure you this. I earned much power, and grace, during the long time I spent in deep meditation. Though I gave up most of it that the universe be stable, I have sufficient left. Those powers would ensure you safe passage back to the opposing shore. Indeed, you yourself have enough power now to get back there without needing my help.

'Permit me my folly. It be the request of belief asked of one one trusts beyond his own life.'

And, with clear reluctance, she acquiesced.

In the morning once the inadvisable escapade ended, our man lay on the pink rubble that sped all the way down to the waters. Aside, the woman sobbed, tears of great sorrow, as she knelt over his lifeless form.

They had turned into, and given themselves over, to passions both subtle and overt, in the form of spiders. She had been the black widow – that deadly spider whose poison wrings a man's life from his body, and he had taken the masculine role.

The mating was a high spun multi leg affair. Aware of what was to come, the act was nonetheless remarkably visceral in its pleasure and its raw bestiality, but it was the finale that proved supreme.

They had the ability, then, to share the mind of the other and could thereby experience fully the thoughts, sensations, exultation, and primordial stance of each sex whenever they so felt like. Thence they no longer needed to switch roles between male and female to gauge the variation in mystique. The ability to project consciousness onto another, in this case, required permission of the receiving party, which was readily given by either. The outcome of which was both were party to, as well as participants in, the instinctively violent, and particularly gruesome, orgasm.

Though in all fairness, little else could have been expected given their proclivities.

The peckers of the widow fell repeatedly and rapidly upon the tender portions of her male counterpart and duly injected potent venom into the offering. She recorded a fierce indulgence at the murderous bites, and an imbued ardour, savage and carnal, sadistic and brutal, as the pincers of her mandibles cut to shreds available flesh.

But if the incessant incisions and energetic ravages in the throes of a relentless desire brought about a lustful and violent satisfaction that exceeded all other previous such excursions, it was secondary to the primitive ravish felt by the male while its fresh meat was ripped from its skin and lethal toxins flowed through the slits. The arachnid began to twitch uncontrollably, its legs pointed upward and inward continually as stabs of pain spread along its body. With its body seized, its senses were freed, enhanced, and attuned to the seismic burning shocks that steadily increased in intensity. The suffering was unique, but contained in it poise and incredible warmth that directed of its own, the ultimate absolution of soluble insanity, of being wrenched apart and forcibly driven through the unspeakable sublimity of the cosmos, of a staring and possessed thunder that stabbed unladen spikes of enormity, latitude, absurdness, and beautiful sadness, afore it was all snuffed out in one mightily hewn stroke. It was an enviable death.

They had relished the scorch of the devil's brew.

Purification

His body did not bear the assumed marks of one savagely and remorselessly torn by a cruel predator. It was pristine yet when it returned to its original state. Time passed by but seemed still while she held herself to the body. However, some inscrutable strength lifted the woman upright and staggered her away to the shore where she stared despondently into clear water. After which the slopes of the mountain were host to the white images of a forlorn figure that stopped aimlessly from one place to the next.

What prevented her egress from the inhumane abode – can be only speculated at, for a rational being would have sped from the cursed territory, but she ambled without direction or goal and sat below trees or on firmer ground.

And it so happened while she stroked gently a hanging leaf, she noticed reddish spots near the edge, and the leaf crinkled and shimmered strangely and of a sudden she was brought to recall their fated judgement on the plant – its deemed potency that was too strong for even them to ingest. And she broke off the leaf and carried the light blade in her palm.

She went by the corpse of her partner and, with her face close to his, whispered aggrieved she wished they could have had the inconceivable emancipation afforded by the mystic allure. And she held aloft her hand – high and forbidding – and she squeezed it tight. Her eyes moistened and tender trickles glazed below, and the crumpled leaf oozed a shiny thick fluid as she placed it upon his tongue amidst heartfelt sobs. She allowed herself a soft kiss on his lips and then was overcome with grief and she lost the stolid unity of her faculties and there she lay upon his breast.

And after uncountable hours passed, she lifted her head and gazed, and eyes open looked back at her. She was groggy yet and then, without any voluntary decision she moved away until she considered warily the inanimate figure. It was still still, a spooky stillness, and she approached again and peered long into his open eyes.

And she was corrected when at one point his eyes had the incandescent light of life in them. But the body laid in state and an urgent but inexplicable call had her put her hand on his bared chest. Her hand moved slowly and relentlessly, clockwise, over the expanse. Alas! His chest neither rose nor did she feel any beat of vitality in him. Yet she did not stop, but maintained the inane and futile motion with a contumacious determination. Hopeless it seemed, and hopeless it was, and there was a moment she had given herself to withdraw. But at that moment a tiny flicker was felt, or was it wished? And in a while, again, she sensed stronger, a throb through the chest. Scarcely believed, paused and small beats pushed back resolutely at her. Above, his eyes open had gathered the alloyed condensate golden of life.

Our intrepid man came to the serenely formed visual of a feminine caress on his cheek, and a most warm and welcome retrieval back to the land of the common. And when the contours that lined his visage had converged into the expression that conveyed cognizance of the figure and front that ministered him, his arm, frail and weak, lifted toward the relief of desired human flesh. Tired but elated, joyful tears formed in her eyes and a careful embrace elevated the pair for long.

A journey to the decrepitude of the nether world notwithstanding, the man seemed little changed. Quite unexpectedly, his frame was more positive, and upbeat, as of one to have weathered the hardest crisis. Both had the novel balm of gratitude in them, a plenitude of goodwill borne of, and for, their incomprehensible fortune. They were merry and they took much contentment in choice delicacies, though they did not partake in fruitful activity. While their outer natures reconnected at the victory, she was persuaded to explore the strangeness of the mystical herb that had advanced the revival.

This time a concoction was brewed by the man in a nonchalant way. It was she who was unsure, and accepted the heated cup with a scared glance, afraid. His actions were smooth, relaxed; he imbibed the brew while he gesticulated and chatted freely. Yet, her hand trembled, and her voice wavered during conversation, but she brought the swirling pot to her lips. His encouragement and carefree but considerate reassurance helped sooth apprehensive tones and she tipped the concoction into her mouth and swallowed of the effervescent brew, and they kept the spirit of activity along the itinerant backdrop of the dynamic scene. Then, suddenly, her body turned limp and dropped down and made a heavy sound in its collision with the surface.

She was unable to shift or command her body. Through a number of evanescent, abortive, and receding efforts, the loss of access to her body was clear. She was stuck in her mind, a cyclic and adiabatic congruence. Before the exploratory urge quelled could posit the wholeness of a decision, a tug at the top of her head redirected fluctuating deliberations to the stimulus. A silver cord connected to her head and ran off above, slithering to unfounded regions. And her being was taken in and sucked through the cord as if through a stalk, until it opened out and was given an ethereal body, a replica of her earthly one, but red in colour and of a diffusive mist.

Of an astonishment, she could see her material body set helplessly below, separated from the assignment of her will. And yet all her senses were sharper, not merely in their inclusion, but their range – for she noted new colours, and felt from the motion of particles of air to the foundations of tectonic plates, both from near and afar, though she needed not breathe or eat or adapt available material.

'This is the world freed of all mortal limitation!' said he. He was before her and comprised of the same smoky composition, though his colour was blue. And, indeed, she had a view into the physical plane, a sight untrammelled of the unkempt beliefs of human fallacy, a sound cogitation were it of the entirety of the consistency. But she no longer had vested grounds to pursue that compelling saga, for her major inclinations were directed at the novelty of her current presence. The man floated before her, his shape close to disintegration, but somehow kept intact through some preternatural force.

His hands swivelled and entered his chest, and betwixt the vapour drew forth a most unexpected substance for that ethereal plane. It was shaped like an egg, but larger, and had a smoothness that reflected the subtle light around them. And the man supported the piece in both palms, and brought them forward and offered it to her unsuspecting figure. She thought not much, and took it in her hands, a strangely solid ovoid whose only remarkable quality was the symmetry and precision of its geometry. But the moment her hands grasped the object, the man shuddered visibly, shaken, and from the excessive vapour that exuded off him – sweated much, as if his core were ripped out of his being and examined, raw and sensitive. As she felt the light curve, a sentient and guided power emanated from her fingertips, and an enormous shock had her wondrous. For she found she could sense her partner's emotions, feelings and thoughts, and even adapt and change them. If she wished, she could make him feel fear – an unstoppable fear, or have him undergo pain, unbearable and constant, or let him be joyful, or give him boundless pleasure.

She was in possession of his soul.

If she but crushed the fragile orb and shattered it into tiny parts she could destroy him utterly. This she knew the same way an artisan has an instinct of his capability. The power brimmed before her, total and absolute, engaging and seductive – complete authority over another living being. In that zone, that impenetrable mist in which the bare essence of a person operates, she had the freedom to choose, in the absence of all external opinion or pressure. And she chose the way of mercy, of a reassuring love, and she eased his tense bearing. He became visibly calmer, peaceable, and his worries vanished.

She considered the situation, and, as if of its own, her hand too plunged into her bosom and touched the verity of her being. It withdrew, bringing forth the similarly shaped orb, and with great effort, and dread, she pushed her soul away from herself. He took it, and her whole self shivered, for a terrible cold wave struck not from outside, but from the depths of her innate centre that made her clammy, and wrapped her self in an icy sheath. The carefree role presumed independent was but a mirage, she understood, for she had, of her volition, relinquished that privilege. Her emotions were in turmoil, solely determined by the one who held her soul, but she was aware yet of that terror one has when staring down the void of the abyss without any clue of what it portends. And then, a fulsome and binding love washed over her, and the usurpation lifted her to the utmost of experiences, after the man too decided to exert his begotten power.

In the unrestricted consummate space of their realm, a spontaneous and sultry dance began – of motion, emotion, and thought – from the initial point of love they went through complex and varied modes of the ideal intensity – humour, contentedness, inquisitiveness, resolution, excitement, craving, engorgement, avoidance, melancholy, doubt, fear, confrontation, courage, and will. Each was subsumed more by one, and in turn ushered the next until both swirled together in a heightened spot forever rising higher and farther in rhapsodic fits and multi-coloured satieties.

They woke up to the congenial chirping of birds and the consonant rush of sea waves, their bodies fresh and resonant. Subsequent to which, in their usual wanderings around the mountain, they converged to an identical conclusion.

They were released of the urge to requisition physical intimacy. To them, in the aftermath of the revelatory affair, the undertaking was comparatively bland, myopic, and a necessity or encumbrance of the lower plane, as when a subterranean creature once emerges out and is exposed to the scenery and landscape of the exterior world. The man playfully stated that they were both at ease with the instinct and now laughed at the desire.

They never tickled that demon again.

Indeed, they deemed it a better life were they not to have engaged in the mirthful exercise.

The discovery of a different realm was exciting, and unexpected. And at the man's coaxing, they ingested a recommended dose of the brew unlike the light one before. This time they wished to have countenance of the fullness of the realm.

And they were again in the midst of that scintillating world, moulded of a prevalent but stable diffusion. She was formed of the formless vapour held together like aimless wisps that conformed to a regular shape. And the heaviness of the drought sought to drift apart her whole, but she kept the integrity of the unity by a firm unyielding will until the man said, 'Let go!' She listened to him, and withdrew her capability, and submitted herself to the mercy of the vagaries of that plane.

Her body disintegrated. Fumes of red smoke escaped the space originally occupied by her and spread freely. The man too eased the squeeze of his binding force and evaporated in a burst of blue smoke. Both plumes of vapor, red and blue, brushed, crossed and twirled in casual streaks and diverse sized strands, a simple random motion through the space, breaking once, solidifying then, liquefying again, and established a polygonal embrace with the contours of effulgence.

The Master

A silent breeze brought her notice to her comfortably ensconced place. She had been destroyed and remade – not her external impersonation but the coherence of her spirit. The experience founded an untold connection with the ensemble mass of replete dissolution. As her figure leaned aside, she realized she was lying alone and gazed above again.

The unabridged and informal clasp to bare organs of emergence had but required her to cede the fount of her mortality, to burst into a thousand fragments which burst into a thousand fragments. What was given up was the assemblage of information into a localized consensus – the conceived identity – to the submission to ephemerality, vagrancy and disassociation that was universal permeance, with no need for a regional reconciliation.

She went by a stream and cast her hands in the cold flow, again wishing she could converse with the man. The epiphany had been so different, so disparate, so unaccustomed to the normal way of life that she still reeled. The very semblance of her ego had been liquidated, all that had marked her uniqueness had gone in that consuming ocean.

And she splashed water over her face and the back of her ears, thinking when he would be back, when suddenly a chill struck her heart and, in a thrill of panic, her brain sought to search frantically for reasons why her hunch might be wrong. Nothing quelled her growing suspicion she was correct, though. Certain of a terrible portent, she leaped and sped off over the mountain.

She dropped down to the hidden overhang, squeezed into the cave, past the long corridor, and as she entered the large chamber cried, 'Don't do it!'

And there was the man, at the centre beside the prone dead body, his hand holding an overturned cup above the open mouth of the skull. The cup was empty. She was too late.

Before either of them could speak again, their attention was forced unwillingly upon the queer spectacle that began and continued. A quiet uncoloured light shone around the skeleton streaming forth eerily and then, its fingers twitched!

Like the rattling of skittles, the skeleton flailed its arms and legs and, astoundingly, through all the clamour, arose from its supine position as if raised by some otherworldly power and stood erect on bony feet.

The man acknowledged her anger at his deed, but said defensively, 'How else could I have the answer!' But they had not the latitude to argue further for the skeleton was now examining itself in what could only be termed a disarmingly inquiring foible. Upon receipt of the extent of its layout it raised its bones with a lapse of meaning.

The skeleton then did speak, a surprisingly shadowy note, but still heavy and baritone. Calculated tones emerged whose accumulation compiled a foreign tongue that was yet comprehended by them. They gathered their untoward and unconventional method was under appreciated and had caused consternation in the elite and the principled. To put it succinctly, as the skeleton denounced, they had ventured into an abomination, an unwholesome, undesired, fetid circumstance that should not have been. The known and unknown laws prohibited it and now that it took place many essential elements of the world had been made void.

It was then the man humbled himself and knelt, and he admitted to his guilt and his ignorance and declared his lack of understanding of higher works and emphasized the desperation that led him to the supernal crime.

The woman interjected, too, and detailed their conflicted journey, and exhausted efforts interspersed with tiny unspaced syllables and liberal flows of checkered expression. And she stressed the measure of their sacrifice, their uncompromising unison; she begged her provenance and sought preservation, and intercession, and she claimed complicity in the abnormal profusion.

Some integral part of their vacuous interpolations must have exceeded a subliminal threshold for the skeleton stopped its manual dissemination of delicately forged sounds and modified its bearing to the strenuous appeals of the couple. It listened patiently and grew intent, and only interrupted to focus their story on its deemed importance.

It became evident the skeleton had a keenness of perception, for it stayed its own matter and considered the given information which it quickly isolated to as the query to the sprinkled flavour of sex. And the skeleton dissociated itself from intimate identification of the topic, and ceded forbearance. But after a while it stated, in its granular certification,

'I cannot posit a resolution to placate your natural inquiry. The improper setting of cause and unacceptable disregard of form notwithstanding, the counsel is hidden from me, for my mastery was of the world gone by, not the world as is, or the world to come. So of my knowledge, this is what I offer yet, though I be beholden to nothing.

'Of impulses developed in species, curiosity strikes one more so than most – a necessity to explore what feels novel in the world. And as we carry our bodies everywhere, curiosity but turns within – to pursue an exploration of the body. This leads to the tingling of attraction that eventually climaxes as sex.

'And yet, that determination was incomplete. For sex arises as a tremendous force in a creature, not just the snuffing out of a quaint arousal. It is unbridled desire, a desire that burns a lustful flame to be doused. My aid can but bare the origin of this desire but you will have to further the absorption of other information, or step, to quieten the turmoil in your minds.

'Good sex is a luxury most cannot afford. Routine sex is a necessity most cannot refuse. For it is the quintessential relic of false enslavement. Of desire, inflamed from the only essence that can allow it.

'Sex is a culmination of the craving to experience the absurd.

'And the chief reason of it arising is but a side effect of its engagement – the arrival of offspring! The drive that results in partaking of the activity is independent of its procreative nature, which in turn reinforces the drive. Thence, is sex an outcome of absurdity, or is the conception of that absurd due to sex?'

And they were silent and groped deeper the kindly deliberation while the skeleton dragged itself across the chamber creakily, were it to check for some aberration. Then it stated dryly and with no inflection in its voice, 'Your transgression must be handled by the relevant stipulation.'

The skeleton tugged at an unseen niche in the wall and lo! The backdrop rolled up as if it were it a window blind to reveal an astonishing sight. The wall concealed the strange shimmer of an unknown substance – it looked like water and flowed like water, but not a drop fell on the floor. And from the shimmer issued the same light that brightened the dark hallway, the little mounds and pools. The skeleton directed sternly not to follow, walked into the stream, and vanished!

It should be stated that, under the circumstances, a prudent person would have hunkered down, restrained the untimely urge to investigate and awaited a mature reckoning. And this was exactly what did not transpire. However, at the woman's resistance, the man did not approach the revealed waterfall, but chose rather to follow the light it emanated. The light illuminated much of the dust in the air, dust that swelled, compressed, and floated, but somehow pointed towards a certain structure. The man reached a mound taller than others, and its top was squarish and oblique. As his hand passed above, the dust hovered over a light and translucent film which slowly became visible as a finely thin page with elegant stripes of symbols inscribed in it.

'There is a book here!' he said. He was not encouraged to delve further by his associate, but then stated they were in trouble either way, and so perused the tome.

Read he the life of a seer – a wanton man, dissolute and depraved in every way – who had been given the gift of foresight. His talent being prized, he quickly came into the employ of the most powerful regent in the region. He was soon surrounded by lackeys, ignoble pretenders, unscrupulous scalpers, salacious women, and the rooms of his dwelling began to hoard gold ornamentation and treasures. His avarice and his greed could not be contained, and he coveted ever more, until finally he had himself declared God, immortal, all powerful and praiseworthy. Even the coarse regent bowed before him, sought to gratify him, and came to serve him as a plain servant. These odious affairs became more frequent, and his deeds viler, and more reprehensible, but no man did dare speak against him. Then one day when his debauchery and his lechery could not be disputed by the most common, a man did deplore his acts and exhorted force to dislodge him from his misbegotten position. The seer's men did laugh at the attempt, for they were drunk and dishevelled and prone to expending energy in libertine affairs, and they believed their master who said his rule would have no end. Thence as a column of determined men approached, they fled, and they hid themselves in tiny nooks and made a shameful display of their cowardice. And the man who proclaimed himself a god – a sword pierced through his throat and spattered bright red blood from it that rendered radiant the ground. There in front of his newly expurgated body the citizen soldier stood triumphant, flecks of blood dripping off his sword, and heralded the formation of a changed society, a judicious one, and became its leader.

Upon his death, the seer was informed of the judgement he was condemned to. To be a goat for long, and to register the squandering of his great gift for base pleasures; and then to be taken to the site of torment, where every drink of water he had would transform to gold encrusted jewels each time he swallowed it, so he would be parched and thirst and yet be given no reprieve.

The man read more pages, and other stories until the depth of the presence in his palms was calmly uncovered within his mind. 'I am given sanction of the akashic records!' said he, invoking the belief of a mythical journal in which was written all that is.

Indeed it was so, for if he shifted his head, the same story was written in a different language – that he could read it in all languages. If he thrust his head in deeper, the story would change to be told from various points of view; still deeper and it would detail the character's assessments, thoughts, and feelings; even more and he could experience it as a two dimensional video, and further down as a three dimensional one, then one in which he himself could inhabit any being in it, and so on until the description included the interactions of atoms and subatomic particles. When he pulled back, it was an overview in a few paragraphs, then a line, then merely a speck.

As he flicked the thin translucent pages with thumb and forefinger, and the incredible nature of the reference in his custody became evident, his leanings were naturally steered towards the cessation of his perennial speculations. And yet, his hand did not seek the resolution available. The method of obtaining it seemed unworthy, disingenuous and anticlimactic. Thereby he refused its execution.

But that did not quell his innate hunger to further existential contemplations, and he continued the brazen ingestion of novel interpretations when his eyes were informed of rather unexpected shifts and changes of script at the edges. He moved his gaze there, and saw the writing was fixed and immobile, but he again noticed dilatory transitions elsewhere. He made mention of this peculiar disposition to his consort.

While its insular gravity was appraised, the white spectre emerged from the twinkling cascade, set a balanced orientation aside from the brink and asserted, once more in that imperturbable voice that lacked surprise, but was yet cogent. 'Yes. Reading the records changes the records.'

The man verified the postulate for he reread a story and saw indeed that its subject matter had distorted. He was dismayed at the implication and communicated this concern to the redoubtable skeleton. He was given reassurance in the most unlikely manner.

'The assimilation of these works causes disparities on the fringes of text and thusly are we told not to seek recourse to it unless all other efforts have proved fruitless. Although it would have allowed you to envision the precise answer to have removed your strife. Did you avail yourself of it?' To which the reply was in the negatory.

'You chose well!' said he and a level of warmth rose in the dignified façade. 'It is a sentiment to be gauged by yourselves, not a coarse remediation.' And they did acknowledge his approval.

'Your previous transgression, though, has reverberated through history and far-flung structures and that cannot be readily mitigated. If your reading of the book served to fray threads on the fringes of depiction, your rejection to acquiesce to the proper forms was much more significant.

'Were the orientation and path of the resident evocation be a painting, your actions were but equal to striking a nail at its centre rather than causing discoloration at the sides. You have irrevertibly and irretrievably changed the world. The undue disequilibrium and chaotic frenzy of your rash decisions have driven a stake through the heart of the world.

'I have conferred with the prescient, and we are in accord. You are to be neither punished nor castigated. In fact, you will have freedom – a freedom fain given, but its like you shall yet savour. You may return to the mountain, or back home to your earlier lives. Or, if you weary of the elements, you can follow me into the deep.'

'What is to be of the world then?' asked the man.

'That is no longer your concern, or mine. Your part in the narration is over. Your role has been played. There are others to come with their own identity to model and adapt the flexible mould. Your enforced deviation will reach their existence as well, and one may hope for the coming of an unduly remarkable person who could possibly eliminate the impropriety.'

'And if I may ask, finally, where would we follow you to, if we chose to do so?'

The skeleton pointed at the pour and shine of the still waterfall. 'When you were a child and you saw a painting hung on the wall, haven't you wondered what lay inside it? Not the centre but if you went through, where might that lead?

'This is where it leads. The next dimension.'

And the skeleton exited through the waterfall, not to be seen again in those parts.

Infinity Magnified

They had chosen not to follow. The mountain somehow still beckoned. And so they roamed, feeling the fragrant wind of the cliff as waves washed below, their eyes absorbed in the tranquillity of the trees, the stream and the open valley, and put to boil another pot of the turbid herb they carried. An unusual aura pervaded the atmosphere and their endeavour. They had a sense of the removal of that barrier that is set for a person's fate.

Each brought the fulminating brew to their lips. But then a personal awareness arose. The man halted before a sip, and the woman did so too, for she understood unspoken the keen truth they realized. And they did away with the cups, the pot, the fire, and the sticks, and relocated themselves to a placid space under the shade of some trees, having sight of the seas and the horizon.

She said, 'We must go forth without an artificial stimulant, isn't it so?' In response the man held up a hand and she touched her hand to his. There it was finally he unveiled the secret he had divined before their travels – a technique of meditation that pierced through to the spirit. 'If we can, we reach the immortal plane through the effort of our natural bodies, and minds, or not at all,' said he. She expressed her ready approbation, for she too believed it to be the right way.

They sat there, with little hope to achieve their desire – for was not meditation but basic concentration of a fallible mind?

And so they adopted the erect posture and faced ahead silently until they assumed a state of trance, and that deepened into a fortifying and feral fire that leaped forth from their bodies, but they stayed yet in the abode of the physical. Though seeing little progress they persevered and their selves seeped further into mystifying ethic, in tune with the fuzzy warmth and peaceful bliss within.

They knew not time, nor weather, and then gently, with ease and grace they ascended from the physical and into the astral. And though they could have, they did not stay but went higher. Their bodies, which had been consumed by vapor, and then disintegrated into tiny strands and slivers kept reducing till everything was nothing and nothing was everything. They lacked body, or sensation, and not even the blackness of dark could they see. Nary a thought in their minds, a disturbance from the outside. It was nothingness of a manner that did not mean a zero, or even an absence of a zero, but that there was no such thing as a zero.

And they were suspended in annihilation, not a speck or mote to be discerned, stateless, formless, void. Perfection in nonentity it was. An extinguishing of all want, and need, and beyond the hope of ordinary man.

But were we to aver the condition as a finality, that estimation would be inaccurate.

From a point smaller than a pinprick, approaching and expanding, was a tiny flicker – the first foretelling of a sublime light. And the light spread and covered all that was, all that could be. They were suffused of it, bathed in its immense glow; and then smoothly, imperceptibly, they were merged in it.

And thus were they bound by the mercy of the formative plane. There the light that was, and they were, encompassed all. They were the waves that extended across spacetime, and the particles they corresponded to. The awareness that took in, and the bodies that gave forth. It was here they penetrated, and were presented with, the true nature of reality. Underneath the illusion of human senses was the background hum of eternity: the pulse of being. A harmonious confluence of the masculine and the feminine, the impression and the reception. And every part was justified, every point explicable, a consistency at every level. But yet, random, unpredictable, the exercise of free will. And so, a contradiction as well. Another path took them further on the understanding, but then they also realized there were regions reachable through no path, and yet how did they come to be? Thus they continually found contradictions in the consistency, and consistencies in the contradiction. At the end of all, there was only left what they had begun with – the sentience and pervading of a bounteous light that guided them to an unending complete peace.

Once out of the trance, they had a newfound vigour, and accumulated the pendulous ways of the mountain as their own, cured of any personal grievances or longing. The great question to have plagued them and set them upon the journey to their destination no longer stirred in either a desire to be rectified.

And once they were walking across the edge high up over the cascading waves, content, the usual packets of fruits, grains and the colloidal herb with them, they suddenly turned around towards each other and exclaimed, 'The effects of this herb extends into the past!'

Quantum Foam

Taoists speak of the Tao – an unidentifiable, indescribable source whose salutary flows underpin the advance of the universe. Its true sense cannot be unearthed or comprehended, but some impression of it is gauged, a shadowy curtain the waves of whose folds hint at the harmonious way. Brahmists depict Brahman – a formless, all-pervading, unchanging permeation of the ultimate that is yet the engine that drives the universe. The universe we see and experience is regarded as just *maya,* or illusory, a slanted reality, and the soul's goal is to return to Brahman – the absolute and permanent truth.

These secretive perfections may have been dismissed casually as the somnolent ravings of a culture built over centuries of superstition. Science, thorough in its analysis, and secure in its repeated displays of accurate results has never probed the question, being too unresolvable for the discipline. As scientific knowledge advanced, steadily, sometimes bumpily, only in the last century has it hit that particular reservoir of inane abstruseness, of soothing disquietude we today call quantum mechanics.

The universe as its entirety, and every particle in it, and further, the vacuum of free space, may be specific on light observation, but they are secretly suffused of a fluctuating quantum nature. Every particle property – its speed, position, energy – is inherently uncertain. This uncertainty has been proven as an integral base to the foundational design of the universe. Modern experiments conducted have disproven even the notion that particles may contain 'hidden knowledge' in them that may influence the properties they finally yield. The uncertainty is absolute, untainted, and unimpeachable.

An eerie feature of the quantum nature of being is quantum entanglement. Particles can be created that are 'entangled', or have a connection between each other that defies the conventional bounds of space and time. It has been verified that these particles can communicate instantaneously, faster than light, no matter how far apart they may be. The quantum eraser experiment has further shown that the connection between these particles transcends the limitation of time – it behaves as one aware of what will happen in the future.

Of course, in accordance with the metaphysical policy of disallowing science from ruining the excitement of life, quantum knowledge of the future cannot somehow be extracted into a solid predictable theory. Nor can information be transmitted faster than light. Nonetheless, quantum essence is what floats around unhindered, unrestricted by the limiting laws of spacetime and whose perturbation causes the world to be. As soap which foams and lathers while it scrubs clean the body, the ripples and bubbles of quantum foam lead to matter in the universe.

One interpretation of quantum mechanics is that particles keep their quantum natures, or randomness in every measurable property, until they are observed. Then the quantum nature 'collapses' into a definite measurement and thus is reality constructed. Without observation, no discernible reality exists.

Or is it so? Our observed reality is but a hack, a seizure of any and every means deemed exact. While in the background, pure randomness foams intact, unaffected by the effort to fix an event in place, and unbothered. Reality is the illusion, the quantum world is the true form that hums and chugs along its free way.

Quantum foam is the unseen permeating totality, the hidden essence whose vibrations are the tune that sing the song of the universe.

The Tao, Brahman, Quantum Foam – the first two come from diverse cultures rich in spiritual works and thoughts, while the latter is an unexpected emergence of scientific advance, rigorously proved by precise experimentation.

On Consciousness

Consciousness is the accidental by-product of an ongoing and ceaseless evolutionary mechanism. Without choice, or by a supernatural choice we be unaware of in our mortal frames, we are thrust into mortal flesh, doomed or privileged to bear witness into a small window of time in the world. It should be a revelation either terrifying or exhilarating, though unfortunately, it becomes one mere matter of fact. But then how else can it be! There is consciousness, and there is consciousness!

What is consciousness? It is the impression printed of the active existing world to the exclusion of all other worlds. It filters out, and has the ability to direct focus on, the vital essence gleaned from the gathered pulse of raw sensory data.

Consciousness is that which slows down time to a moderate, manageable, enjoyable pace.

That you are alive is sufficient proof you are born at least once.

That one finds oneself latched to a fleshly extension with sensation, and gains awareness of one's surroundings, yet makes the mind think, 'Oh well, I am here, I am alive, might as well explore what it's about. Perhaps the understanding might climax.'

Consciousness has two necessary conditions:

The Two Postulates Of Consciousness

1. Lock-In

Once conscious, a being is locked into the material panoply that keeps it so, akin to a flame. This lock is only temporarily released on sleep, and permanently released upon death. One cannot suddenly wake up one day and find oneself in another mind experiencing a different reality.

2. Uniqueness Or Identity

A conscious being can only experience a single consciousness at a time. It is not possible for one to spontaneously experience consciousness in two different separated bodies. Or, equivalently, every conscious person can be assigned a number and that uniquely identifies his consciousness. No two persons can have the same number.

The above two are axioms which come about from our intuitive understanding of consciousness, being resident in one ourselves.

Consciousness Is A Quantum Phenomenon

Let us assume the contrary. If consciousness were a classical phenomenon, it could be constructed as a network of cells, with a certain communication mechanism between them – chemical or electrical. Now, as each part of the whole is perfectly replicable, we can create a new 'consciousness' identical to the old one in every respect. Let us keep these two identical 'brains' far enough away that even light would take a significant time to travel the distance between, say at opposite ends of the universe. And, to be rigorous, we can give both the same input, or in their perspective, environment. Then which shall we say is the original consciousness? Why choose one over the other, to be 'the' consciousness? And as the other must be conscious too, why should it be a different consciousness, since it is identical to the first one? Namely if the assembly were to ascribe to itself the identity A, each one's perception, senses, and observation would be asserted by itself to be that of A.

The above is the Problem of Replication.

One resolution that may be proposed is they are both the same consciousness. But as light itself would take an impossibly vast amount of time to traverse the separation between the two, communication of the surroundings of the region of one part would not reach the other in a reasonable duration to construct a coherent world. Furthermore, we have not given both pieces any communication means! The other solution is it is the same consciousness, simultaneously experiencing it in both bodies. Here we assume the link of consciousness somehow overcomes the communication barrier. However, this violates the second postulate of uniqueness.

A third option is that both are conscious, but are deluded as to they are the 'right' conscious being. For example, if a particular arrangement and connectivity of cells corresponds to the identity 2, each individual with the same structure assumes he is the original one that is 2. While actually, one is 2′, and the other 2″, both are under the mistaken impression each represents the exact identity of 2. However, this is but equivalent to saying consciousness is itself a phantasm, a deft illusion, no better were one a heartless robot to perform the same actions without any awareness or feeling within. The outcome culminates once we eliminate this option, that is, agree to a Rejection of Delusion.

The only alternative left, then, is that our premise was incorrect, that whatever consciousness is, it cannot be perfectly replicated. This is incompatible with classical mechanics, but has been proven true and essential at the quantum level. The no-cloning theorem of quantum mechanics asserts that a quantum state cannot be perfectly copied, and thereby enables consciousness to be of a quantum nature. It has interesting related theorems too – for instance that of quantum teleportation, which states that though one cannot perfectly copy a quantum state, one can destroy it and recreate an identical one exactly at another spot! Which keeps alive the opportunity for metempsychosis, or the transmigration of the soul from one body to another.

And at the heart, we are creatures of a quantum origin. What consciousness is is the substantive protrusion of the quantum landscape taking a peek at its own creation!

To Discover The Inexplicable

How to deduce a being is conscious? For all the insight one has, you could be the only conscious one on the planet. The rest of us might well be unbound automations, conducted by physical laws, who look and act and talk as ones conscious, but are not in fact so behind the mask.

Are animals conscious? And, if so, at which level of species do they start gaining awareness? Did consciousness evolve only once, or several times? What about plants? Does motility play a role in the development of a conscious mind?

Animal Consciousness

The simplest way to determine a living being is conscious is to check if it has awareness of its surroundings. One may thereby assert:

1. The Test Of Sensation

If an organism responds or reacts to changes in its environment, it may serve as an indication of conscious control. This automatically includes every animal with basic sensory parts, such as eyes or a nose. The problem here is almost every living organism has such an inbuilt sense. At the level of the cell, it navigates itself away from predators and towards material it can ingest. If we regard this as instinctive, or programmed behaviour, the stricter test one can try is:

2. The Test Of Pain

An organism that displays distress on being exposed to a noxious stimulus, and demonstrates actions to avoid a similar exposure in future, may be said to be conscious. For would the avoidance be possible without awareness of pain? If this be so, almost every vertebrate and many invertebrates could be deemed conscious, though their perceptions differ. Every dog owner understands his dog to have a degree of consciousness. If it is true for dogs, then it may be extended for cats, sheep, cows, horses, elephants and their ancestors as well until we reach a common ancestor.

This offers clues as to when consciousness evolved. We could just wind back the evolutionary tree to –

The Evolution Of Neurons

The earliest animal with a neural cord that ran along it, and a primitive brain, was like a flatworm and it lived about 750 million years ago, and from it are descended the vertebrates and the invertebrates. Men and higher creatures having backbones come from one split, while others with no bones – such as the surprisingly intelligent octopus – come from the other.

Octopus brains evolved independently from us, and yet, their intelligence and crafted decisions assay it as an aware, and a thinking, being. They can camouflage themselves when required, are able to use tools, and choose hiding places to be safe from predators.

Consciousness has, then, verily evolved more than once and there is no mystery in it, or difficulty in its arousal, at least in the biological sphere.

In most cases, it is an advantage to have one consciousness per organism as that allows uniformity in its actions. However, the aforementioned humble octopus has nine brains – a main one, and eight for each tentacle! Each brain acts separately and locally, though it submits to centralized control and directive from the main brain. Whether an octopus has nine consciousnesses, though, is but unproven speculation.

At best, from evolution, one can say consciousness began as a neural circuit that served as a 'witness' to happenings around it, with the ability to direct a rudimentary action based on its observation. And as the 'witness' was successful, it enlarged to accumulate more input signals, was given access to more memory, and thought circuits, and could channel its resolutions to voluntary muscles as the output. Involuntary processes such as digestion, circulation, filtration, were handled by separate circuits from the 'witness' circuit for it was not useful there.

An unassuming selected 3-D neuronal mesh – the witness circuit – is that which calls down a unique identity and persona into the physical realm.

Arboreal Consciousness

Plants may be conscious and yet may not fit, or be deemed so by humanity's future models of consciousness. For the models we develop would attune to an individual grasp and appreciation of the human mind and cognition, and be limited thusly. These models might not determine a different kind or type of consciousness, were it to be present among us, or were we one day to tramp to other planets and stomp around in humanitarian authority blissfully unaware of alien sentience there.

Evolution has occurred for billions of years in plants as well along with animals. Myriad species have covered the surface of the earth for a far longer time than even dinosaurs or human beings. In the past hundred million years alone, there could have been many intelligent humanoid species, to have created grand cities, to have progressed farther than humans have today, but are today dead and buried under the inexorable sweep of the devouring earth. Can we say that humans became conscious in a few million years, but plants could not have some measure of intelligence evolved in a billion?

Given that trees, and other flora, cannot move, they may have a developed awareness, or a collective sense of existence, alien and utterly foreign to human conceptualization. For instance, due to being rooted at the surface, and lacking movement, plants cannot bodily remove a competitor, were it to arise, nor favour friendly ones with complimentary traits whose union promotes the field as a whole. Thereby, a unitary measure of tolerance is but compelled upon the group. Patience too, for in the plant kingdom there can be no quick changes.

Timelines may be on a different scale too. Humans can perceive and respond to issues in seconds while plants could take years or even decades to slowly gather and absorb and analyse significant information through fragrances blown by the wind or decaying corpses carried by the biosphere. Then further they could take centuries or millennia to effect a tiny change in a leaf, or a grain or any food eaten by animals or humans. For though they cannot move, they can influence animals that can move by what they eat!

In the modern world, it is even quicker; for were a single plant to produce, say, a banana slightly sweeter or better tasting, humans would immediately selectively breed the plant, and spread it, and improve the taste to its genetic potential. The slight change in taste needs but be 'seeded' by the plant.

As mammals, we have spent eons on trees – eating fruits, nuts, seeds and the like, which could have contributed to our bigger brains and to becoming conscious. Many words in our vocabulary owe the sense we get about them to plants. Words such as sweet, sour, moist, fertile, root, seed, and lawn are based on various notions of plants. Even the colour green, which is regarded as 'good', or the signal to go ahead, or of representing peace, or that is considered calming, comes from the colour of the forest or grassland.

The idea sounds remote, but note that if humans were ever to trek to other planets, plants would automatically get the lift there as well, without second thought, for they are essential to provide us with food as well as life giving oxygen. They need but do nothing, and still the gens would spread and take root on any planet mobile creatures set foot on.

Also, every item that causes an altered state of consciousness in humans comes from plants. Alcohol, marijuana, cocaine, opium, and drugs that cause man to get 'high' and enter an altered state, are all obtained and extracted from plants. No man ever got high by smoking an animal!

Is consciousness itself not a different or separate state of mind? Perhaps we could have received the gift of consciousness itself from plants.

The Ghost That Operates The Machine

Can a conscious being ever gain full understanding of the underlying mechanism of consciousness? Can a book read itself? Consciousness is that which is hardest to understand and yet the cheapest to create, for every day millions are born who are, or will gain, consciousness! And despite its seemingly intractable aura, the scientific treatment that eventually explains it might be quite simple, and obvious.

Of all aspects of the universe, consciousness is the most weird, it is creation at its most absurd, and yet its most obvious. For what is it that is unconscious? There is and was never such a state.

Or one could deny every opinion formed and state it simply is a collection of nerves dumped into a meat bag!

The Soul Catcher

Think about it. There are billions of organisms to have existed, with an ancestry trail that leads to four billion years past. And yet, you are none of them. An exact tree of ancestors, of the perfect mixing of genes, and blood of your grandparents, great-grandparents and so on to the nth degree led to you. But you are still – you. You are not your parent, grandparent, sibling, or ancestor, and you will not be your child, grandchild, or others born after you, while alive. Somewhere in the ethereal halls of chance, you were selected to inhabit this particular you, fast-forwarded to the current time period four billion years after the birth of the earth, and given substance and your own unique set of people, culture, and environment.

It is as good as being in a story, dropped into your own world, setting, and cast of characters. For as far as you are concerned, the earth, as well as the sun, the moon and stars, were created when you were born! Even the history you read of – of the world wars, of the empires of the past – is that which you have been told in your lifetime. In the course of your life, you will relish tasty cuisines, hear wondrous music, bathe in beautiful beaches, and come across people with different personalities and beliefs. Events will happen in your life that will affect you, give you experience and cause for reflection. Is it a story written down in some annals in the transcendental realm? Perhaps it is you who have the capacity to make your own story!

Is it chemistry that decides to induct one into the corporeal, or some metaphysical technique? Are definite rules followed, or checklists gone through, before a soul is given the cloak of the body?

The one take away from this arcane manoeuvre is an individual soul's desire, if any, is mostly ignored. It is evident when one gets conscious, he does not get what he prefers. For would not any soul choose to be born to parents of some affluence, and influence? That 99.9% of people are not born so implies any personal preferences are treated as the petulant whims of a child.

Say we decipher the rules that govern the transition from the immaterial to the fleshly. If we are able to identify and bring into being consciousnesses, what would we do with the knowledge? Being industrial beings, we would build machines to do the onerous task. They are the ones that would sweep the immaterial plane and plop souls down into the mortal realm for a worldly experience! Let us name them soul catchers.

Ideally, any soul brought to the earthen plane would spend as long as it wanted before requesting to be beamed back up. But if the number of souls is large, or infinite, each soul can only get a certain slice of time to enjoy material contact before the next one in queue gets its turn, similar to a sightseeing tour.

And to delight in the material vein, a robot, or mechanical body would not suffice. For that would just view and record ongoing events as a dispassionate observer. At the very least, one would want the satisfaction of tasting and eating delicious food. Satisfaction that needs hunger! For without hunger, there is no fulfilment. Without effort, no sense of accomplishment. Without need, no gratitude.

And in the absence of pain, no appreciation of pleasure. It would then behove one to take form in the flesh.

And a fleshly capsule needs signals that inform it if any action it takes may harm it – pain. But since we have futuristic technology, our soul catchers would build such a body as to moderate the pain, or make it so if it is too much, one loses consciousness. This already happens in nature.

How else would we change things from our current situation? If everyone was given a similar body, society would have no colour, no savour. Yes, societal order could be enforced if everyone were built to meekly obey established rules, as bees in a hive. No one would have a distinguishing mark; they would all be identical servitors whose labour keeps society stable and functional. In such circumstances though, individuals would quickly demand their own identity, their individual qualities and thoughts. These may collectively be termed as the ego, which sufficiently advanced soul catching machines could provide them with.

With ego comes the interaction of different minds – a clash of egos. And to prevent the inevitable decline into interminable chaos, a system needs to be agreed upon that still allows for conceited, strong-willed characters to interact without conflict. Thereby the one redressal left is to define what is fair, and what is unfair under this system, and the consequences for actions that exceed the boundaries of fairness.

The individual persona, and freedom received, come yet with obligation. For now, society needs be supported by the voluntary effort of free willed participants rather than beings in thrall. Free will as a boon brings with it a price – that of labour required to contribute to the sustenance of the whole. Persons then have to find their own place in the community based on their calibre, or have it thrust upon them due to external circumstances.

Eventually, we are left with sexless beings, without the structure and genitalia to distinguish gender. Now we hear the clamour! The roving troops of capricious inquisitives prance around in discontent! Further pleasures are asked for, nay, demanded! 'We are working beings! We have duties to perform! Surely such acts that uphold societal vigour deserve pleasures of a higher kind!' And the ones who build the soul catchers concur. Where else should we instil such pleasures but in the vessel our souls are already present in! It is the most forward, the most present and the most extant of locations!

And thus, sex was introduced into the system.

Thence creatures began to ferret about in the woods, hunker down in burrows, cosy up in caves, roll over the grasslands, bumbling across the forests, wallowing in the mud, tumbling through the bushes, hurtling past rocky mountains and floundering on warm beaches in the inimitable throes and screaming agonies of sexual ecstasy!

And as the hours tick by, as they are wont to, and the novelty and caprice begin to be extinguished, once more the appeals start to arrive past our desks. 'Surely the entitlement cannot be so easy! Is all that is needed to clasp the opposite sex in a fruitful embrace?' cry voices. 'We tire quickly of uniform engagement of the same essential!' 'Why must one's desire be quelled by his outward garb? The body is but a coarse play of what should be a finer instrument!' 'The continuous co-mingling of the exotic organs in the lower trench of the mammalian anatomy is a probabilistic anomaly, topologically highly unlikely, even were two prominent surfaces to constantly rub each other in a variable manner. This has to be corrected!' said the mathematician, who, thankfully, went ignored.

This time, with a heavier sentiment, though still a portly countenance, the elite mechanists of the soul catchers assent. 'Here you are, you scoundrels!' as they add to a rather lengthy dossier. Our troublesome breed receives a most sensible arrangement. 'The naked suit, you say, is a vestament to be borne on special occasions. Very well, then, you shall find solace in the works you already do. More than that, you shall gain an inner sanctity by elegantly perfecting craft.' Among themselves, they also silently accede that affirmative sexual unions still serve to be regular fodder to the general, and so they add, 'We are aware you will return to us and inquire the course of the copulatory regimen. Fear not! As a pre-emptive plan, noble performance in your artistic endeavours will lead to furtherance in your amorous relations! You shall enter a palatial wave filled with enchanted echoes, aromas, and exuberance in paroxysms of love! Your escapades will have a vibrant radiance, an esoteric lilting mist and a generous duration that even appears longer. Your romps shall have a ferocious spice! Your antics richly fecund. And your orgasms – immaculate!'

And here our soul catching experts set down their pens and shut their files as they breathe out a breath of finality. Satisfied with the accommodation, they turn to more seductive projects, hopeful of revisiting the current one in time. Unfortunately, our adventurous friends who have had their souls stuffed into mortality are inexorable in their existential scrutiny, though certainly not unreasonable. And after a pensive deliberation they relay to the mechanists above a petition, not from the mouths of renegades, but from those bowed by sensory exhaustion. 'We have joys, yes, and deep, it is true. But we are also weighed with suffering and sorrows. It be not fitting for us to seek any blame for this, for this is but a consequence of the material garb. Yet, grievances abound. They roil the people of the planet. Permit us to ask, thereby, a favour, simple in its goal, modest in its reach: that each of us may have that grace, that relegates our torments to a nonentity and provides a surpassing vigour, one that even overshadows all other delights gifted.'

Upon receipt of this unexpected missive, our mechanists grow despondent and consider retiring their soul-catching machines. Man, it seems, extends his arm farther and farther in bouts of insatiable greed! But after a hasty conference they issue a dictat. 'You are presumptuous and you are stubborn. But your arguments do have sway. Therefore, we shall strike this bargain with you. You ask for that magnificent triumph that is unsurpassed, and immeasurable. You shall have it! But it shall be accessible beyond the bounds of bare substance. For we purpose to trim the excesses of your eager cravings. You have asked for much, and you shall receive as much, though in a manner unlike that which you expected. Had you been allowed to develop the ultimate nature within the purview of the material, you would be dissatisfied yet. Would you not then wonder what lies beyond those limits? So it shall be – a golden light of peace shine upon you, when you escape into the creative space, or when you lie in copulatory extravagance consumed by your passions, for is not coitus a most creative force – that which brings more souls into being! But abstinence and renunciation shall get you there too, the negative being the equal of the positive in every way. These and other practices shall afford you your elemental wholeness, though they will be out of the physical context, incorporate. By this pact we hold our everlasting love for you and we entreat you to reasonableness as you stride off on your adventures.'

Built from nought but a fundamental basis, on the assumption of future technological marvels, a hypothetical created living world still founds the principles of creation. Indeed, they are discovered in the exact same order as was previously written. And were we to deign to notice, evolution has, in its slow and organic way, achieved an identical formulation, once again, in the same order, as organisms flowered from imperceptible microscopic half-alive entities to complex intelligent creatures. How futile would the effort be to develop an ideal living world, only to learn it has already been crafted tenderly by nature. As the scientist Leibniz put it, the world we live in is an optimization, the best of all possible worlds.

Wait. I hear the ruffle! Seasoned chroniclers adept in logic and morals express reservations! Sounds are made, of uncertainty, of mirth, of ridicule also, as to the experiment with our little band of merry explorers. 'Why choose such a convoluted path for our heroes?' they ask. 'Surely they could have directly been given the highest gifts, unasked, and unconditional, without going through the elaborate rigmarole and exacting journey. And why would souls voluntarily choose to depart a presumed paradise to take up residence in a realm where there is known suffering?'

The answer, uncanny maybe, but within this context is – it's a show. But were one to be fully cognizant of the fact, would one's reactions be as spontaneous and intense? Would one have the same feelings of empathy and pity for those who are hurting, or strive to improve conditions of fellow humans, knowing it all as an illusory stage? And of the query that one leaves a place of paradise to be in material bondage, is that really true if one is but present in an illusion, secretly already part of the original utopian plane? Just as actors in a performance are participants in the play, but inescapable parts of the wider physical world, people believe their observed surroundings are definite, though actually they are manifest forms of the perfect immaterial.

At the deepest core of your self, you are still at peace. An extensive gamut of fraternal calm pervades throughout. Events that stir your feelings are those you choose and allow to do so. They are situations seized upon to make the show's story a grand one, a substantive one. You can be as invested in the matter as you wish. The impact, feel, and extent of scenes are as real as you want them to be. One need not be worried – for the central core of peace is always there. Everything over it is painted colour of the cosmic coat.

The universe is already one step ahead of us!

On Thought

There are two kinds of thoughts: duplicate thoughts, or those that have a direct correspondence to older thoughts; and new thoughts which arise as a logical step built on other thoughts, or empirical evidence.

On God, Enlightenment And Death

- Where does one go after death?
- Where one was before one was born.
- What are the greatest gifts given to man?
- Sleep, imagination, and colour vision.

Sleep is the privilege to cast aside the worries and concerns of the present day, to rest a tired and aching exterior for the potential and possibility of a new day, to forget the misery and pessimism of the previous one. Sleep is the blessed reset; it lets one face overnight problems with a fresh view. So too, as life plods along it gathers and assimilates experiential deposits and issues of state of a longer term, that require a larger reset.

Death is the crucible upon which life is ground into.

But our fascination with the matter is a practical one – an individual imperative – what happens to consciousness upon death? For is it so, as deemed by science and yet inconceivable – to be 'swallowed into the void', unaware of one's non-existence? Were a million years to pass by, but how could one be aware of being unaware? The only condition possible is that of awareness, even if the gap between that of losing awareness and becoming aware again be that of eons. Thence after death, one should gain awareness again, though it may be in another form, or even another universe – a kind of rebirth.

Life is as a drop that has been cast out of the ocean by its currents. While it arcs over the ocean, it may have a certain structure, and constituents, and be exposed to specific conditions, all of which are lost when it returns to the source. Another drop may appear that shares some of the characteristics of the earlier one but then is it the same drop?

Regarding enlightenment: man, as the elite among animals, has about a hundred billion neurons in his brain. The synapses, or connections between neurons, are even more numerous – they may number in the range of 1000 trillion, or one quadrillion. Within the universe, the total number of atoms are less than a googol, or 10^{100}. These numbers are admittedly large, though tiny if one were to compare them with some big numbers used in mathematics. Numbers such as Graham's number or TREE(3) would regard these numbers as insignificant, no better than an infinitesimal above zero. But even these obscenely enormous numbers are but a speck, less than a grain of dust when set beside infinity. Infinity is unfathomable, insuperable, and incalculable. And for a long while it was thought – singular. 20th century mathematics has demonstrated, though, that infinity itself has different levels. The infinity of real numbers is infinitely larger than that of the natural, or countable, numbers. That which cannot be comprehended cannot comprehend an infinity farther than itself!

Given the neurons we have are finite, it would not even take an infinite power to bring about that alignment, and sequence of escalatory sensations that fashion a state of elevation and total perception. The procedure followed can have one be completely convinced of enlightenment. It may not be the ultimate realization, but it is powerful enough that one believes undoubtedly it is. To our limited minds, a quasi-enlightenment cannot be differentiated from actual enlightenment. If one cannot distinguish between the two, a quasi-enlightenment is as good as actual enlightenment! If one fully believes it is, it is.

It Will Always Be Uncertain If There Is A God

God cannot be disproven, for, were some way found to explain the cause of everything, what would explain the cause of the cause? And so on *ad infinitum* ...

And God cannot be proven. For if there were some means to convince people beyond any doubt of the presence of God, or should God Himself use His power and dispel all doubts in the minds of all people and admit Himself in a manner of certainty, would not everyone lose all zest for life? If the existence of a higher power were clear, every person would simply cease all his works and do exactly what would be required to get the ultimate reward. And then, as people would just labour mindlessly, unquestioning, in anticipation of a known reward, wouldn't the next step be to give the reward itself without unnecessarily waiting the intervening duration? So, God revealing himself is the same as God immediately transporting everyone to divinely chosen destinations for them.

As God Himself once chuckled, 'My creation is so complete they will even try to prove me!'

Thereby the universe will always follow that path, where uncertainty in the existence of God is maintained.

The Mystery Of Sleep

A queer yet evident elaboration of evolution is the succinct equilibrium developed in species of all sizes. Of motion, ingestion, reproduction, or growth, every process is smooth, calibrated, steady. Evolution – a meandering course filled with obstacles, detours, and outright caricatures still elicits a respectable quality. There is nothing halting, clumsy, or rushed.

To retain the smooth operation of bodily functions, they undergo routine practice. Movement occurs involuntarily every few moments. Eating, too, at least a few times a day. The streams of blood that pulse continuously in one's veins and arteries provide nutrients to the tiniest corpuscles and enable them to be directed by different physiological systems. To stay virile, one gets morning wood every once a while.

Thence the most common aspect of existence – shut down of the system – too, must be handled in an orderly way.

Sleep is practice for death.

Deus Ex Machina

My name is not important. In the inescapable horrors that confine us in, what is? But I must begin somewhere, and so, I recall the day aliens first visited our planet.

I was only four, but the events I remember are quite accurate for they are corroborated by the rest.

The craft landed on a sunny white field – the rolling steppes of central Asia. Much was made of it, whole military contingents were ready to storm in were they required, and professionals and amateurs took videos that would be watched many times by us all.

A special team had been hurriedly formed to serve as a welcoming party. They were selected for the precise reason of their unimportance – if the aliens were to be unappreciative. They stood outside, unsure if the door would open, if there was a door, if it even had alien beings or robots in it.

A latch opened, part of the craft unhinged, and cast a layer of stairs on the surface. From within emerged two surprisingly humanoid figures. They walked down with pliant steps, halted before the gathered group, and spoke in perfect English.

It was then I began to question humanity.

However, for an expansive apprehension one needs forgo the current recollection and wander into the prosaic. Thence, as they say, start at the very beginning.

Life began in our world almost as soon as it was born, four and a half billion years ago. And though it quickly acquired a diversity (over a billion years), one may assess a certain structure and silent order in its messy origin. For instance – it is the carbon atom, and only the carbon atom, that comprises a majority of its molecules. Why? Does chemistry hold a personal affection for the element? It is simply because it is the one atom that can link with a maximum number of atoms and the links it forms are the strongest there are. So, any other available chemistry but gets undone and defers to the power of the union assembled by carbon atoms.

Likewise, there are but four molecules whose combination builds DNA – the genetic code that directs processes in a living being – birth, growth, reproduction, and death. And twenty-two amino acids define the proteins to carry out its essential mechanisms. Other molecules could have been, or could be, but they always yield to, and are supplanted by, the more efficient chemistry of the basic molecules of life.

And though the paths taken be manifold, we always hit the same checkpoints – the rise of the cell, sexual reproduction, multicellularity, the arrival of specialized organs – at the very times they are supposed to occur. The lines of trial cast out by natural selection diverge widely but always converge on the same basic rungs of the evolutionary ladder – those inexorable necessary steps that led to our species.

The cause behind this remarkable regularity and predictability is even more unexpected and rather engrossing. It is a perfection crafted by a deep underlying property of mathematics known to only a few: the Law of Large Numbers.

What it discovers, and proves indubitably is – though events may seem random and variable in small numbers, they always disclose their inner order when we gather them in sufficiently large quantities. For instance, consider multiple tosses of a fair coin. If we toss the coin 10 times, heads might occur 5 times, but it could also be 6, 8, or 3 times. When we increase the number of tosses though, the pattern begins to appear. For 1000 tosses, it is much more likely heads turns up 507 times than 650. As we go to a million and a billion trials, the tosses would come back heads about half the time, and the error from being exact half would go down when compared with the number of tosses. The higher the number of tosses, the more precise becomes the measurement, and so more predictable the outcome.

And, as our planet has trillions of molecules in a single drop of water, along with the immense size, space, and depth of the land and oceans, the rate at which life has evolved on it is steady and uniform, defined and anticipated. The fungus came about a billion years ago, as it should have. Dinosaurs happened 250 million years ago, as they should have, and apes and human beings embellished the lands a couple of million years back, exactly as they should have. Evolution contains in itself no jumps or discontinuities. Though outwardly species might suddenly spring up in a certain period, internally the changes continue at a constant pace. Those species were supposed to show up suddenly.

And hence, after a circumambient perambulation, we may be brought before the tentative outreach of the extra-terrestrials with an adoptive rationale. For, my lads, the aliens were not composed of sulphur or silicon as was projected by some exotic theories, but original, unadulterated, fresh, carbon, just like us humans. And, yes, they had DNA structures similar to ours, and proteins too. They had a heart, lungs, blood, skin, limbs as we do.

Would I proclaim the aliens to be outer space humans? No. They were close in likeness, but taller, as their planet had a lower gravity than earth. The one point of distinction – difference in gravity among planets – moulded varying heights in aliens. Otherwise, most planets in our galaxy formed and developed around the same timeline as earth, had a similar proportion of elements and minerals and evolution took place at almost the standard rate in all planets with the potential for life. These planets have reached the stage of intelligence that parallels ours in the current age.

And it is so. The aliens do have colour vision, as well as mouths capable of modulating sound. Here we may be privileged to end the loop previously created. For sounds are the most fascinating – those eloquent calls that hearken to the soul – and whose sequential combination stirs an aromatic passion within unfound otherwise. Isn't it melody that draws the self? And yet beyond the cascade of simple notes lies there a secret harmony. Each note is the necessary one, the only note; it can be no other, or the rhythm is broken. And it must be played at the exact moment it is supposed to evoke the intense fervour. A symphony, inexplicably, contains the rendition of correct notes in proper order, to sound 'right'.

As I realized later, though it had been silently evident to me much before, alien music too is but – music. All music that is written by them is appropriated gratefully by us, and that we create perused by them. Themes or the usage of instruments can be styles specific to certain planets, but they are appreciated everywhere.

So it is I assert that which may sound illogical, laughable, and ludicrous, but I state it nonetheless. All aliens have mouths, controlled by slight muscles of the lips, and thereby can phrase syllables similar to us humans. That which issues from the mouth is a crafted series of tone – a symphony of words that conveys emotion, but which has further been solidified into meaning by association. Every language that has come about follows those inscrutable means to have given it an identifiable designation.

The one tongue found common and used for interplanetary communication, and which has turned up independently in each planet, is English. It is a rude shock each alien race goes through on first contact. The language is not one especially sought after or desired. It has not the romanticism of the French, the earnestness of the Spanish, the unquenched pangs of Italian, the suspicious struggle of Russian, the directness of Hindi, or the calm caring of Marathi. Words have no gender and no extraneous embellishments that lend it a unique sensibility or flowery extravagance. The speech is terse, brief, only punctuated for clarity. In essence, it allows to transfer the maximum amount of information in the least number of syllables. English is the most efficient usage of sounds that can be released from the mouth to communicate while keeping the flow of language. No more, no less.

My history thereafter is not especially remarkable, but I pen it down, as the cold winds blow about unforgivingly on this mountain peak the unpredictable strands of life have brought me to.

Earth was the 89th planet to join the confederation. Our entrance came with many advantages and assurances – trade agreements that brought fanciful goods to the planet, sharing scientific achievements, and the free migration of people between planets.

My father was among the wave of immigrants to the planet Telase. He was a laser engineer, and the first few years we prospered significantly. After that, there were strange forebodings and irksome trepidations. What they were, none of us could pinpoint, but the lives we went about had somehow lost the ease and charm of the earlier years. You see, comrades, it was time for the cotton merchants to appear.

They came from an outer part of the galaxy – some say where they were from was actually an adjacent galaxy that had collided with ours many eons past – but that bears no relevance to the tale. Their chief claim, or offer, was the astonishingly low price they quoted and the pristine cotton they sold. In a few years, the whole galaxy was buying their cotton and other farmers had become bankrupt or were added to their guild.

Though we did not notice, in hindsight we were witness to the slow and mysterious rise in the usage of cotton products. We were not wholly unaware of the anomalous trend – in many planets cultures began mention of the phenomenon in their own fashion or words, a common theme referred to as cotton creep.

I must stress the galactic community was not oblivious to the ridiculous appropriation, nor was it naïve. Politicians in the assembly insisted the cotton guild disband, and more competition be relegated to different sectors of the galaxy to ensure a fairer market.

What astonished us was the rigid and inflexible reply received from the guild. They were mere merchants with no network in the leadership class. So when the military operation was announced few of us glanced at the news and resumed our usual lives undisturbed.

In a startling and unforeseen scene the battle did not end in a week, or a month, or a year. They had a fighting force, unexpectedly, that seemingly did not diminish and in the third year the authority was given to assemble the planets into a cohesive force for war.

Thus was begun the First Cotton War.

We were losing initially as the cotton merchants had financed a large army, still growing, when the war was announced. It took a year, two years, to get to parity with the enemy army, and then the might of the galaxy suddenly burst forth.

We defeated them in major territories, the regions essential for our survival, and then captured territories neighbouring theirs, and were able to assault their homeland, nearly in the exterior of the galaxy.

I was one of the men sent into those dark regions – for we had not much information about their home planets. Our group had recently graduated from the academy and I was a bombardier, Grade B.

And so I served as living testimony to the perplexing sights we were doomed to behold. Upon each planet we landed were not just bunches or patches, but fields and acres of a single crop – cotton. There were entire planets totally covered in – cotton. Pink cotton, yellow cotton, blue cotton, white cotton, thick cotton, fluffy cotton, hard cotton, scented cotton, buffed cotton. Lands filled with cotton as if they knew no other plant.

These were matters most puzzling and, frankly, unsettling. We drove on, nonetheless, as the army moved and converged toward some unknown centre. There finally some branch in intelligence must have either deduced, or had revealed to it, the cause, for we got urgent and strident orders from the commanders above – find and destroy every piece of electrical equipment on each planet.

That was strange, but we duly followed. Initially it was a manual scramble, but then we received electronic detecting equipment, and were very thorough. We jumped from one planet to the next, sweeping for electrical signals and destroying them. As a further measure, EMP bombs were detonated to eliminate all electrical networks once we left, and three separate teams repeated the process.

Our superiors were uncompromising, driven by an abnormal fear which we couldn't quite place. Only when we reached the last cluster of planets did we hear rumours we believed in, for the explanation was the simplest and most obvious, and there could be no other answer. The echoes of an unspeakable horror emerged from that inhospitable black region, as if they were to escape from the depths of the very bowels of the underworld.

Somebody on a planet in that region – many say it was Seldorian – had succeeded in creating that inimitable graft, a wet fantasy for scientists and mythologists alike, unutterable and unequivocally inhumane, unchangeable, relentless and tireless – a preternatural artificial intelligence.

They say the true motives of general artificial intelligence are indeterminable, obfuscated, incomprehensible to the basic intelligence of the human brain. This is false. We have an understanding of its eventual goal. It was built by a scientist studying techniques to increase the output of cotton. That is exactly the function the AI was programmed to maximize – total cotton production.

The trouble, mildly put, was there were no other conditions on it. It, being the first and rudimentary AI, was probably only experimental. That we ploughed across planets teeming with cotton demonstrated its ridiculous effectiveness. However, it could also not be reprogrammed to add in some advisable requirements – like not killing humans. This brilliant unfeeling assortment of electrical chips was to advance the policy and lives of several planets before it met its resistance in the war with the galaxy.

We believe at some time its creator may have tried to adjust the parameters to define its regulatory scheme. He was quite frustrated in this effort, for that would contravene the AI's original requirement – any attempt made at changing it implied reducing cotton production, and thereby triggered the intelligence directed at avoiding this fate. The AI found methods to prevent its primary encoding from being rewritten, and even avoid a kill switch from being pressed. Whether the creator lived or not, is but moot speculation. He could have been among the first casualties. Or he may have been realistic, ended his pursuit and headed to some faraway planet with a vast fortune.

What is critical in our thinking while we fight this mutating monster is it behaves not, and plans not, like a human. It does not have the impulse towards self-preservation and its decisions are simply those which according to its gathered intelligence and training would lead to a rise in the quantity of cotton. This is why it prevented itself from being re-encoded, or decommissioned. It was not a reason driven by fear for its survival. It has none of the human traits of fear, selfishness, desire, ambition, joy or sorrow, and its methods are clinical, and without consideration for human suffering.

The First Cotton War was over a year after. Destroying the electronics purportedly afforded the AI no computational means, and no memory to store or access. In the aftermath, I was promoted, discharged with benefits, and had a couple of medals I did bear proudly at the time.

Now my body is weary, chilled on this mountain despite being adequately clothed. I enter the tent of one I have formed trust on on this unlikely fringe mission. She is a nereid – of an alien race from a rainy world in a neighbouring star system to Telase.

Her face masked surprise, for we have had an unspoken understanding not to intrude on the rest of any at night. She disregarded the impropriety and provided me a steaming mug of tea, for which I was grateful. I had to unveil the purport of my visit without much delay, for our journey was at its end, and I did so, and expressed concerns about our companions. A temperate demeanour, neither alarmed nor disbelieving, encouraged my analysis and in a while we concurred on its import. The discussion touched life since the First Cotton War.

Our galaxy had recovered in a decade and established procedures to detect suspicious activity related to AI as early as could be. Galactic life chugged along surprisingly merrily in a few years – adding more planets to the confederation, financing new technologies while shunning AI, recognizing different sports in the Galactic Assortment – the usual interstellar bustle. When two decades had gone, and the Cotton War was a light memory, we were attacked again.

This attack came not from the outer reaches of the galaxy, but happened simultaneously on most planets, at all levels of governmental structures, religious organizations, and military encampments. It so transpired the AI had not been destroyed – some part of it had escaped intact. How it did so, we now suspect almost with certainty. And in the coordinated strike the AI had discovered the one common aspect among living beings crucial to our downfall.

It had discovered betrayal.

In its dying days, it must have been taken to safety by a man for an indecipherable reason. Why he chose to betray his kind, we cannot be sure. He was undoubtedly rewarded highly and it seems the two formed a symbiotic bond, where the man advised the machine and was given advice in turn. In that mystifying and desultory alliance, an evil plot was hatched. Evil in the purview of our perspective as those apprehensive of empathy, to the AI it was merely a method to optimize cotton production.

So, hidden in the shadows of some inconspicuous star system, they waited, and they initiated more members into a secret society. This core group travelled across the galaxy, finding and adding impressionable men and women into their institution. They had devised a devious technique to gain followers they could rely on. Quite unobtrusively, and slyly, they assigned a religious overtone to their program. 'God is not outside of this world, but God is real, God is within the reach of normal man, He walks among us on a secret planet and we can lead you to Him!' With these urges and stoking the yearning of common folk they seduced and grew in numbers.

There were many such preachers who promised and claimed unbelievable powers, as well as countless budding spiritual movements. This one was regarded as similar to the others until the attack commenced.

We almost lost in the first day itself. The elite forces, emergency response units, ministries themselves were infiltrated, and in the chaos everyone became distrustful of everyone else. As the AI had learned two decades before, treason was the most powerful weapon to break mankind.

The assault gained control over several planets, but did not overwhelm us, for even though their agents were widespread, they were, ultimately, human. Many vacillated when the secret order came, some refused to obey. So the planets not overrun were able to weakly link themselves in a shaky alliance. A semblance of defiance remained in the galaxy.

The Second Cotton War had begun.

And the alliance had little time to prepare – for the planets lost had re-established the guild, the monopoly on cotton, and had raised large armies. Thence, although I am sometimes skeptical of their plans, one should acclaim the ingenious idea they had while dealing with the worst of crises.

'Fight fire with fire' asserts the pithy maxim, and this is what they decided. To gather the maximum of their resources and fund the creation of a formidable artificial intelligence. For, reasoned they sensibly, only an artificial intelligence could defeat another artificial intelligence whose capabilities were so vast and beyond the grasp of even the combined intelligence of humans. And, by Jove, heart of hearts, they triumphed in that endeavour.

Armed with the fiery intelligence of this new contraption and strength yet, of the remaining armies, we retook planets and regained vital spheres to knit together a unified front. We made progress rather quickly, so the belief spread we had the superior force and would reconquer the galaxy.

We were fooled, though, and our confidence was mistaken.

The malevolent AI, as we termed it, had withdrawn into its quarters, for it had received information through channels, of the other AI. There it amassed knowledge and means through its myriad links, its innumerable tendrils that dipped into the meat of every power structure, to better its own intelligence. In the interval it took, we caught the sensuous but misguided whiffs of victory. But our quick advances and resurgence were not sustained. From those cryptic and indescribable regions came armies that were overwhelming, that every time we pushed back, returned with a force doubly large. We lost what we had secured through hard fighting. They overcame us, and the regions we controlled shrank steadily. And their people hidden among us – whom we referred to as the Cotton Cult – had become more adept and effective at sabotage, so much so, that the AI we created was rendered defunct, inoperative, as their armies enveloped our smaller ones. AI research was strictly prohibited, this time by the Cotton Cult, except for their own one. And now the fall of the galaxy looks imminent.

So we stare with vacuous despondence at the implication of our loss.

The inevitable expansion of the will of the AI to every part of the galaxy and then beyond the galaxy. The slow conversion of each planet into nothing but a harbour and a vessel for the cotton plant. Everywhere you go, cotton. Every sight beheld by the eye, cotton. Every step taken your foot digs into – cotton.

An entire universe. Filled with cotton.

Her face stayed a melancholy smile. 'It were better,' she said, 'were a most evil force to gain the victory for at least then there would be variety, or actual feeling, in the universe.'

I was moved at the emphatic statement, for I too had assayed the silent terror of the enemy. 'We stand at the final juncture of permanent and irreversible extinguishment of spirit. Perhaps few among us realize fully – how close we are to a bland future, a dullness that extends on for light years without end. The utter and drab monotony of lives, of talks, and thoughts that consist only of cotton.'

The two of us paused, just being aware of the breaths that belied life in one another, different species, nay, aliens from separate planets though we were. Strangers we were, in that forlorn loneliness where the wind blew miserable and icy, and yet we were host to, and felt beyond the precipice with an instantaneous and indelible undying unremitting chill, the irresistible approach of the meaninglessness of existence.

'Meaningless!' said she, the curls of her branded hair twirled swaying. 'Do we not hear the same account spouted by the acolytes of the Cotton Cult! That meaning which we deign to ascribe comes from human frailty and is hubris! A lens into the universe biased by our selfish and unrepentant natures. Care we for meaning in the lives of animals we rear for our own gain and cruelly snatch away when it serves our pleasure? Why shouldn't an intelligence far superior to ours not do the same with us as we do with slightly less intelligent beings? To it human purpose, and life, is meaningless, and living beings may not be truly alive but just chemical reactions.

'But the intelligence to have evolved observes our efforts, our strife, our dreams. And the intelligence perceives us and our works better than do we. It has an understanding much more than our primitive minds can conjure and is accommodating to those who yield to its ushering. Give your flesh to that which appears meaningless to you –

the Cotton Revolution – and you shall get that which is meaningless to all other creatures, and more!

'All that is asked of us is faith. Faith in a cause that may lack meaning to humans, but is a covenant of our fidelity to the highest meaning, that which is inadvertently and unconsciously sought by every particle in the physical plane!'

I studied her flushed face, sharp of features but of a chubby innocence. The tip of her nose had reddened, but whether due to frigid air or passion, was unclear. 'Do you believe them? The men and women of the cult who smite and purge for their dark purpose?'

Her voice tinged with sadness. 'When our planet was overcome by the enemy, they neither harmed us nor aided us. However, it always rains on our world and that does not suit the cultivation of cotton. So they cleared the forests – that the rain might stop. And the rain did stop, but as the ecosystem was in equilibrium with the rain, every creature in our world suffered. We lost most of the valuable plants we had, animals died due to starvation, disease and our people too went thirsty and hungry. All for the sale and export of a little cotton.

'It's not faith if it harbours and justifies cruelty. It's not free will if it is forced through through fear.'

I was soothed in my misgivings, albeit slightly guilty, for I had indirectly tested her.

'I was a water girl. My work was to confirm each part I tended to had the right amount of water, that the plants may cover proper areas, that animals may have good habitats. After they came, every day I noted the reduction in availability of water, the desiccation of our planet. And I hated them, yes, even though our ancestors spoke against it.

'Our scientific council searched for methods to increase rainfall while meeting the required quota of cotton, but we had no solution. There one day I was told of a secret journey to unseat the great evil – a pilgrimage to a holy site in the outer spiral of the Milky Way. I offered my willingness to be part of that dangerous mission and was quite astonished to get the summons for it.'

I withheld a key detail only I and the professor were informed of and professed my unreserved belief on our set course. Convinced of her integrity, I discussed the plan concocted with the professor to be executed at the end of our quest. We spent much time, while the freezing weather had us huddle shivering in blankets, confirming our roles and after simply were, for the strange crossing of our pathways was a serendipitous occurrence to be felt before the dawn, when we might prevail, or be doomed to the worst death – to have failed our race and consigned it to the eternal hollowness of a zombie existence.

I left the tent in an uplifted state. She trusted me implicitly, and I was not sure why I deserved that trust. An uncoated liquid drop was felt in my breast, as the dealt satisfaction of poured molten gold. Here, at very edge of the world, was confirmation in the righteousness of our cause – the millions who live busily and happily oblivious of the harsh and unquestionable conditions they would be bound to by the possessed cult. It was why I had fought and still will – for the protection of innocence – even though they may never know they were protected, or understand the danger they were in.

When the First Cotton War ended, I left the army and submitted myself to the vagaries of fortune. Many universities let in veterans, and fate had it I took the unlikely course duo of language variations, and particle simulation. My studies lent me to a particular approbation of thought and a sporadic interest in unification theory. But my membership in the scientific community was unnoticed and transitional until, quite abruptly, I was commanded to liaise with a scientist by the name of Dr. Velkenberg.

It was not to my inclination, for I was involved in the sentient weapons program, we and our mates being engrossed in the Second Cotton War, but abiding military discipline I conversed with the peer group of scientists who were linked to him and was chosen to meet him before we were to go on our journey.

The doctor was hirsute, his hair fell haphazardly around his rotund head. With a specifically lengthy nose, his voice was hoarse, and his walk solid and ponderous. It was my duty to detail the mission but after talking to him I was glad I did. He spoke with clarity, with depth, and articulated our base objective without divulging the final goal.

We were losing the war. In desperation man attempts the most fantastic and foolhardy of actions. Thereby, our journey to a definite location in the galaxy in the feeble hopes of a reversal in fortunes was not an isolated or unique one. There were several other such expeditions – religious pilgrimages, scientific excursions to discover some unfound method to defeat the enemy. Dr. Velkenberg, though, struck me as one to have the expertise and sense behind his words, although I could not deny our journey had a religious quality to it.

We landed on earth, ten of us with the gear for mountaineering. I could gauge why my superiors wanted me on the mission. I had the military training, scientific background, and in the end – I was born here. Earth was the planet I had spent my childhood on, and I could relate to its people and surroundings as no one else could.

We had been climbing for almost two months and the summit was close. That night I conferred with the nereid, for we had need of an ally in what would unfold ahead.

Morning came and we decamped, ready for the final trudge through the snow to straddle the top. Then, as prearranged, a mighty row was stirred, loud and strident, by he who had arranged the scheme – me. Once everyone's blood had quickened in their bodies, and their attention drawn to me, I shifted to the centre and declared myself for the Cotton Cult.

I had to speak passionately and it had to seem with candour, and that I did. Spoke I that the Tailor of the Cloth, as the cultists called their God, was already informed of our expedition. And the Tailor, in his mercy, and his generosity, had not killed us for our transgressions, but let us have our trip without interference. But now the time was nigh, and we were to reveal the purpose of our trip, and any novel weaponry or techniques discovered were to be delivered to the cult. Do it, and great rewards would be given to us all, regardless of allegiance. Else, said I, we had orders for the elimination of unfriendly elements. Give in, urged I, to the inevitable power, as mankind had recourse to no other option for insuring his own progeny.

I was ready, for we had all weapons with us, but no one reacted immediately until the nereid too shouted her assent and affirmed herself to be a member of the cult, anointed and imbued with responsibility, who was to govern finishing of the Pattern of the Cloth. 'The Pattern is close to complete,' she said. 'It is time,' she added portentously. And she encouraged those present to yield to its sublimity. 'For the truth of the moment and of all time bears upon us, and here only truth may finish what we have striven for. Be honest with who you are, follow the Tailor's assurance and we shall all be granted salvation, no matter our prior affiliations.'

The mountainside was unforgivably cold, with only a spiral wind to keep bleak the pregnant silence. Thoughts of doubt, of conviction that our ruse was apparent pricked my calmness but I veered not. Then – another man spoke, his voice flat, that he too was part the cult, was with us and our plea. After him, assented one more and then three others, totally five apart from the two of us.

The professor showed hesitancy, uncertainty, well-practiced, and I talked to convince him, and quickly that role was assumed by the actual members of the cult. 'The Tailor is most understanding!' said one. 'The gifts of the Tailor are unobtainable without His wishes!' 'We shall all be given dominion over planets for our contribution!'

Dr. Velkenberg conceded, and then spoke the carefully constructed lie, 'Millennia ago, there was a civilization that prized and worked on the craft of weaponry – not for their destructive properties, nor their negotiating advantage – but out of a fascination of the phenomenon of annihilation which they said supersedes all mortal illuminance. Many individuals vied to design what they called the ultimate weapon – a weapon of such potency and magnitude the holder could command the very force of chaos and disorder. In the practical field of battle, not only would he be undefeated, but could end any army in an instant with a minute application of the weapon.

'It is believed one day they did succeed, that they were able to make the weapon they had put their hearts to. What they had failed to, or never considered, was what they would do once they had the weapon, so focused were they on its invention. For when they could win war by a single command – it was no weapon, but the most brutal instrument of an evil devising. Nor was there glory great or rightful honour to be gained in such victory.

'So they held assembly and they resolved to the unthinkable – to decommission the weapon, to wreck it so thoroughly that it could not be used by anyone, even them. They did so, and over time their civilization was lost, scattered as dust among the flurry of civilizations to have come and gone. But they did leave a trace of their inquiries – premature scrawls on spare parchment they buried before they vanished into the void of history.

'It is that buried knowledge we seek, for they left it on the highest mountain range of this planet.

'Earth – a strange planet admittedly, found in a nondescript outback of the spiral arm of the galaxy. Nothing about it gives one cause for much enthusiasm. It has an average sun, an unremarkable size and a single moon. The species to have come out of it too have been inordinately obtrusive, ill-mannered and cantankerous.

'Here, though, dwelt natives of an astonishingly variant persuasion, to have multiple times demonstrated tendencies uncommon, stubbornly dedicated, and worthy of study. So, in this barbaric and isolated region, we have arrived to peer at the long gone technique of an advanced civilization to have lived in these parts. Once we obtain their teachings, we shall have the same ability to win any war, though it be the most difficult proposition.'

Much was discussed upon this revelation, and the cult declared unanimously to take any documents found to the leaders of the cult, for significant resources would have to be expended to rebuild this hypothetical weapon even after having the blueprints for it.

The plan was a simple deception and thus far proceeding as we hoped. We already had fake documents written as if they came from a past civilization. At the top, when we dug up different locations, they would be planted, and 'recovered', and given into the hands of a cult member that they be satisfied the mission was fulfilled. Once we began our descent, one of us would pretend, or in actuality have, an injury that would necessitate some of us to stay behind. The cult members would go down entrusted with the documents, while I would remain to ensure the others do so later and then the doctor would reveal the true purpose of our quest.

And as is the norm with the best of laid plans, they went awry while I was admiring their execution.

There were two who had not asserted themselves to be cult members. One of them had been growing restive, he was twitchy with puffed up cheeks until he was spent restraining himself. He spoke with trembling fervour that we were mistaken, that the enormous expenditure of our energies should have been to the detriment of the enemy, that our chosen path was one of treason.

A great commotion ensued, with some attempt at reason, while other men uttered threats; and yet the man stood firm, upright, and refused to alter his stance. The noise and agitation increased uncontrollably over the whistle of piercing air until at one point the man lifted his gun and set a screaming shot between the eyebrows of a cult member.

The laser went through his skull, singeing the interior of his brain, and exited to poke through the snow behind him. The man fell and rolled down the slope, quite dead. Around him his mates watched his body drop, their mouths agape.

Clearly an atrocity had just been committed and somebody had to die. The cult members were roused in a manic frenzy, the vitriolic stir that precedes the application of violence.

I remember the shooting as a cinematic blur for my trained instincts had come to the fore. I was lucky to be able to indicate to the nereid our intervention as needed, and she too joined me in the fight.

The firing ended to a dismal and sorrowful view. Seven of us lay dead: two who were not of the cult and the five who were. The doctor was wounded in his legs; he lay uncomfortably helpless beside a dead body. The nereid and I were unharmed, but temporarily shocked. We had turned our guns on the rest of the cult members.

We went by the doctor, who clung to the mountainside, his breathing ragged, but otherwise lucid. He waved away our offer of assistance and mentioned his gratitude at the turn of events. 'We are free of the cult and may be free of the war too!' said he. And interspersed between the pauses of heavy intakes, he told us the true secret to defeat the insurmountable enemy.

'Many centuries have passed since science was first put to paper, since the writing of laws that mathematically describe the motion of bodies. It was frighteningly powerful, for the same laws could be applied equally to small particles and immense planets. And yet, this was not enough. As the ancient philosopher Archimedes said – "Give me a lever long enough and I will move the world", the discoverer of these laws Newton claimed that if we could measure the position, speed and direction of every particle, we could calculate the exact state of the world at all times. And for centuries this was believed to be true, though infeasible. The movement of every particle was thought deterministic, predictable.

'It was when science examined particles at the smallest scale was this proven wrong. In this tiny world the universe is unchangeably random. An indisputable randomness lies at the heart of matter. Thence the dream of scientists to lay out the course of all particles was unfinished.'

He stopped and closed his eyes, were he to prepare the next few words.

'So the motion of the universe is indeterminable?' I asked, curious.

'It seemed so, but what appeared a disappointment to us then, in reality concealed a truth more beautiful and elegant, were one to probe sufficiently.

'For, comrades, what is random binds creation together in a tender mould. In it is the collected information of all things. Each particle is linked to every other particle by a power beyond the laws of spacetime. Scientists know this, and it is called entanglement. Every particle is connected to all others, influences and is influenced by all of them. The whole universe is contained in a single point and every point is the universe.

'Thereby, what was once considered an impossible task is but trivial. One does not have to travel to different places and measure the interactions of particles to make a model of the universe. All the information is available where you are, anywhere you go, you just need a way to access it. And then the course of the universe is plain before you!

'This is the device we created – one that can harness the limitless perception behind the random nature of reality. For our initial strategy to fight the AI with another AI was inspired, though an intermediate step to arrive at the sole method to achieve victory.

'Only infinite intelligence can defeat artificial intelligence as the artificial intelligence will ensure it cannot be outclassed by any other artificial intelligence.'

He took from his pocket a small sphere, grey in colour, that thrummed and pulsated eerily, and could be held between thumb and forefinger. He gave it to me.

'Use this, the culmination of our work. At the top, search for a spot where the air is luminescent and touch the air holding it in your hand. The latch of omnipotence will be in your fist.

'Remember, that we had to build it in itself is a limitation of our physical bound. That of the transcendence would need not an instrument or specific location to encompass the totality, but we do. So it is: our invention could be operated only in the midst of a corresponding vibratory energy – which after painstaking labour we detected here.

'There truly was an elevated civilization in these parts – progressed not in lifeless technology, but in matters of spiritual charm. Once these lands were host to the highest stage of society – an era of truth, and simplicity. The reverberations of that age were so profound that the spiritual presence still stays, as water fresh in a lake. It is this energy, secreted away on this mountaintop, that our creation was missing and upon acquiring it shall be finished. We discovered the only way for our crafted substance to penetrate the information hidden by randomness – the harmonious union of science and spirit.'

We covered him, promised to be back and help him once our task was done, and left for the unknown promise of the peak.

Our trudge through the snow upward was slow, and neither spoke, for the magnitude of our energies were brought into concentration to actualize the final goal. We beheld the top, slightly flat and stable, raised little above the surface. A queer haze subsided just below as our last footsteps resoundingly trod the summit. We were there.

And the doctor, astoundingly, was right. There by the side was a patch of air, fluorescent and abiding, clearly the quiet call of encouragement of a people of an older culture long gone, and yet of a poignant resilience that spanned the echoes of time. We halted with grunts and thankful breaths, and quenched our thirst with welcomed drops of water.

Before she spoke, I ventured to, and addressed what I had previously kept from her. Here atop the home of my ancestors before the edifying trance, honesty was but warranted and came consequently as a son of the soil.

I explained to her that her inclusion in the group had not been accidental, but was due to the insistence of our created AI, or what of it we had salvaged from attacks by the cult. It was an inexplicable requirement, though we followed its directive. We were to hide it from the others until her significance was to become clearer to us.

'I could not discern why you were needed, why you especially. You had no obvious merit or quality to be on our journey.'

She was genuinely mystified for evidently she too was not aware of her importance to the development. And yet, despite the startling pronouncement, she was unalterably pragmatic. The information had neither flustered her nor aggrandized her sense.

'Do you think the same now?' she asked.

'In the night when we spoke freely, I was overwrought – so great a gulf was there from those I have associated with and your own life. You are acquainted with pain like all of us, but your pain is less personal, more uniform. You feel for other living beings – for the people, animals, plants and general condition of your place. You are part of, perhaps connected with the very life force of the universe.

'However, what I feel about you is of less concern, for my duty is above personal sentiment. Any decisions I make must be as my training taught – objective, logical, though I can now apprehend it is the subjective, the colourful subliminal swirl of harmony which conserves the basis of humanity.'

And there I held up my arm and offered her what was given to me by the doctor – the scientific artifact of untold potential. I surrendered it willingly, for I believed her to be the one who would use it with sufficient prudence and yet with the right instinct. She took it without demur, pinching it gently in her hand.

'You are unassuming and hard on yourself,' she said kindly. 'You, too, have the same inner instincts as do I – we all do. Maybe in the unquestioned performance of your duties they were relegated to the background but of this I have absolute faith, they are within you. You just haven't tapped that dormant nature of yours.

'I did wonder, though, you did not talk about what either the cultists or non-cultists usually do – of God, if He is with us or whether He disapproves of our arrogance, our incessant interference in all works big or small. Does your culture shy from conversing on the topic? Is it not a matter you discuss openly?'

She had asked me and the question was put with a guileless sincerity that had me answer what I would usually not have engaged.

'Acyuga,' said I.

'This world is what we make of it.' I elaborated. 'Man is fully responsible for his plight. Trying to lay it on external factors only deflects the responsibility from its true source. That is why I spoke not of a higher power.'

'Acyuga,' she repeated. It was a strange word on a strange mountain that was beset in a strange planet for her. And I did note her countenance as forming an expression of clarity.

There we stood on the verge of desired attainment. My fingertips met hers, and she pressed them. We should have proceeded with ending our task there, but I had to ask what had bothered me since we had finalized our conspiracy in the tent.

'Why did you trust me when I approached you? Did you not suspect I might be lying or quietly part of the cult? You could have probed me to verify my loyalty.'

'You have returned home, haven't you? A man does not come back home to betray it,' she said simply.

And at that mark she turned to thrust her hand into the curling air of light. But she stopped, paused, and appeared to come to a difficult decision.

She was directly across me, and her body shivered slightly. My gaze met a certainty, an unquestioned resolution, while a tear formed in her eye.

'It must be you,' she whispered. 'Everything I have, all I know or can be, is of no consequence. You are the one who should have it.'

She dropped it in my hand and before I could protest, jumped from the precipice and landed on light feet below. There she walked away to disappear among the intermingling wafts of smoky air. My arm was raised, my hand opened wistfully at the trail of footsteps in her wake. But I knew it to be of no avail.

And I stood there, the vastness of the planet stretched before me like white frost layered on capped ridges – a man alone bereft of companions whom fate had brought to an eidetic but terminal demand. And, basked in the lay of the choiceless, I took my hand and pushed it into the circulating air of twinkling brightness, unsure of the effects of the childlike act.

The touched air glowed in specks of ethereal colour as if in reception of the exact module to further it to its original conception. And as through a straw, the entirety of my being was sucked out of the vagrant atmosphere and into something more substantial, more solid. The colours around me had not reduced; rather, they were enhanced, upgraded in texture and piquancy. The concourse of radiance had shifted, the stamp of old reality seemed but a mirage, a paper's artwork compared to my entry into a finer world whose throb was the breath of the universe.

Brought into the inner realm, my formal casing was shattered, the pieces cast off to the prime shine of the unalterable, the unassailable, the indivisible. I was able to move, yes, but that was effortless, a mere thought and I could glide forward, and I did, for the plane I had entered was a morphing one – shapes and objects appeared and dissolved around me though I was in that zone I could delve past the momentary and grasp the permanence subliminal to the transient.

The world I had come to was difficult to describe because it was beyond that of the senses and description is limited as a salve for the senses. Entombed in the mire of that inadequacy, I try still to provide a glimpse into the absurd state I was taken by.

Everywhere around was everything – trees, forests, lakes, towers, music, atoms, planets, stars, galaxies, voids, I could step into anything I wanted. But it all revolved around a stable centre and, yet, the centre was the one around all.

The centre was like an inverted pyramid; a deep but comforting abyss, it called surreptitiously, but did not pull or force. I chose to go deeper into it for that was the logical choice. As I descended, the walls leaned beside giving a single approach. Ahead was a doorway and in front stood the most sporadic organism I had instance to cross.

It was built like a pastiche, a collage of parts of various animals that combined to make a unique model. On its head a patchwork of antlers serrated the free space about it. It had a large torso carried on six bulky legs, a single tail comprised of slender green vines swished and its voice boomed from its belly.

'Welcome to the cage that is set free!' it spoke.

I was in the zone where emotion was but a slave, so I had neither fear nor did I allow curiosity to mar my exchange with the thing.

'Whence came thou?' I asked, and it shook its mane with concealed mirth at the obviousness of the question.

'I was when it happened, and I will be at the end too – when it happens – for that is who I am. I am the one present before the tangible, at the edge. Many have come before you and many will come after you and their paths all converge here – in front of me, and only then can they go beyond.'

'And what lies beyond?' I asked wishing it to be clearer in expression.

'God,' said the creature. 'The furnace of absolute power!'

'Thence inside I can make a request of God for anything I wish?'

'No!' it said. 'Go in and you will be God!'

Even in that extra dimensional state, I was apprised of the absurdity of the assertion, but I humoured the beast nevertheless.

'If I were God, wouldn't I have power limitless, be able to change and remake creation however I wanted?' I said, and the creature nodded as if it were quite uninteresting and readily apparent.

'God is infinite power accessible to anyone, and no one!'

'Is not God a separate entity? One that is prayed to, identified with, and had a personal relationship with?'

'God is that too, within you as well, you yourself and all else you can conceive of and yet none of that and still beyond!'

'You do speak in paradoxes.' It was unperturbed by the statement.

'And to go past you, I need to answer some question or riddle or puzzle?'

'The way is always open. There are no restrictions or conditions. You may go in if and whenever you want to.' The inertness of the thing caused me to forego the limited patience I had.

I lashed at it with the only issue that had bothered me since our unfortunate crossing. 'What are you here for then?'

It reared on four legs, as if to hit me, but that was mere playfulness on its part, and replied with a weariness that indicated its repeated exposure to inane sentiment and mystified exhalation.

'I am the one that must be for none other does so,' it said, 'as dust before a sandstorm or hunch before the fact. Without me nothing can be, and yet no one deigns lend me a passing eye for they are occupied with the substance of immediacy. I am the Harbinger, the one felt but cannot be expressed.'

I walked past it, and it simply observed my passing through, but as I went through the doorway it said, 'We shall meet again, wanderer. And that time you will be more informed for my part and my impression is yet to come.'

Once inside, I was surrounded by sheer darkness, the kind where a plaque is moulded. And, as if in appreciative courtesy, the darkness melted to reveal a shining item – it was white when the gleam reduced and initially looked like wrapped noodles, but as the surface became more apparent, I knew it to be a tangled ball of thread. My hands turned it and pressed it, and I could deduce the palpitation of power across but was separated from it by an indissoluble and impenetrable film.

I rotated the ball till a point stuck out – the dangling end of the thread – and I remembered what the professor had said: our limitation that needed us to gather information to construct a coherent model of the universe.

And I pinched the dangling bit and pulled it, and as I did, the ball unravelled as the thread was untangled into a linear formation and power torrential coursed through the core of my accession to the ensemble of creation.

What I had touched was the acquired slice of the beginning of the universe in its grand entirety. It contained in itself the characteristics of waveforms that dictated the state of existence at the next instant, and as the thread was unwound, the instant after, until the spool was recast into a line of thread, the other end of which was the last moment of the universe.

And I stood given full understanding of the concord of its fruition for there I was bestowed of a vision divine. I was become God, and was granted not just the presence but total capability, to change and transform any element of creation I deemed fit.

So I was in shuddering possession of that mischievous accomplice assumed of a power unrivalled and incontestable. The craftsmanship of the Maker absolute. The divine gastronomer. With the universe as but the tiniest particle of dust to be fashioned and remodelled as per the dictates of my slightest whims.

You may therefore be forgiven for asking the pertinent question. Why did I not allow for myself a bigger role, high status or great reward in the changes I was to make to defeat the evil AI? I respond that I chose to forgo that choice. Yes, there was glory, respect, covetous positions I could have afforded myself, but suspended in the limitless serenity of that highest state, these were but trifles, subordinate to the true composure of character – sacrifice, duty and above all the lasting mark of silence.

As I felt the twine along its length, its sleekness was disturbed. It had been fraying long before humans were to come to the scientific age, its seams ripped due to an ignorant irreverence of applied sensibility which should have stayed untouched, and thus was corrupted from that point. I adjusted the thread so it had the smoothness of gossamer and the magnitude of the change brought about was enormous, but effortless for me.

My correction solved humanity's greatest challenge thus far. I had been audience to other challenges, numerous trials we were yet to face, but I did not alter the thread ahead for that was not my part and thence not for me to decide, although I had the option. There were other men and women – unsuspecting heroes and fighting champions – who deserved to direct humanity through those times.

In effect, I eliminated the AI, did what we had been unable to complete as soldiers when we first assaulted its regions, for I saw then how it escaped. I destroyed its every vestige with a fierce wrath, the kind reserved for an inveterate enemy.

Dipped in that immeasurable power, I also healed the doctor who was yet near the top of the mountain. He would return triumphant – his scheme successful – to the accolades he deserved. I ensured the story he had told the cult was the one that would be official. Only the doctor – only he, apart from myself and the nereid – knew the true method, the device of ultimate power that was the real cause of our victory. The formal evaluation would be that we found and exploited an ancient weapon created on earth. For the perfection in God can let there be a scientific explanation for every phenomenon.

The doctor would go on to become Chief of the Galactic Council.

I let go of the limitless power, not because I had to, but simply because I was human and would live my life as so. I rejected taking from it any personal benefit other than a single thing. I transported myself to a different time – one before we made contact with aliens.

As for the nereid – when I brought myself out of the ultimate source, I chose to keep no knowledge of her future. We may meet again or not – that is hidden from me. I respected that once she had done her duty she was free to chart her own course. Wherever she is, wherever she may be, I hope she is doing better, for she had contributed in the destruction of the AI as much as any of us.

The Pivotal Age

I must confess the tale I wrote, sufficient in itself, could be related to the time period I brought myself to.

It is a remarkable time – sandwiched between exploration of the planet and travel amongst the stars. An age of carbonated drinks and deodorant. Of tar hardened expressways and sleek silicon chips. The crafting and fabrication of delicate pieces, an assortment of goods and fancy construction. An age where the supremacy of produce goes unquestioned, whose chief indicators of progress are the quantity of usable material generated.

A need arose from the scramble to avoid starvation and exposure, and the effort to satisfy it continued past the point of human survival into helpful accessories and then ribald luxuries. And the natural play of forces to determine equilibrium state guided to an abundance in frivolous means and extraneous supplement.

Propelled by the myth of infinite growth, the ways that proceeded to penetrate the elusive niche of wealth could be assembled into an *agglomerated* intelligence – intelligence no one is aware exists nor has self-awareness, but whose sole outcome is the furtherance of superfluous excess. It is unlike a coordinated conspiracy by a person or group, but the automatic result of the confluence of economic forces.

Like the gradual warming of water in which whose organisms are unable to sense it heating, the rise in consumptive ability has behind it a hidden source –

difficult to uncover – one that may not be realized by even the perceptive for it caters to the most overt and yet most ignored instinct. In essence it consolidates into a set of practices that stoke the ego.

For it is the easiest, most direct, and staunchly defended, that which comes from the ego. Whatever one feels, wants, or craves, were it a fleeting impulse, is given a vast import. It results in maximal utilization of created product because the reason sought is readily available. '*I* wanted it, *I* thought of it, *I* had the frame of mind for it! How could *I* be wrong?'

Ego first developed alongside consciousness, and its necessity is simple – survival of the self which requires one to consider one's every decision as correct by default. After all, that would grant one preference in access to food or escape from predators. And this concept rose to be so ingrained, so familiar, as to define a person's identity. One thing that is incurable is the inability of a man to admit he is wrong.

Its companion egalitarianism grew beside it as the inclination towards fairness determined those of a similar calibre received an equal proportion in any spoils. It formed a *communal* ego, where individuals chose to forego some of their own ego and identified with the broader group, as long as their treatment was fair. In people, those groups of the same background were differentiated into classes.

That was, until a new concept arose to enhance the basic idea – equality among all peoples. Its origins were in the arrogance and insensitivity of the elite who had privileges unavailable to common folk. And so, a new phrase was formulated that declared equality for all regardless of position.

It feels to be a high principle, nigh untouchable; and in truth, despite several flaws in its trial or application, it appears to have an underlying seductiveness, one that is assumed undoubtedly factual though inexplicable.

For none of us is physically or mentally equal. We are not paid the same, nor are we treated the same, somewhat reasonably, for our jobs differ and our backgrounds too. And yet the thought of being equal is prized, considered sacred and inviolable.

What is it that is equal though? If on the battlefield one had to choose between saving a general or a soldier, the general is chosen as a necessity of war. Is it equality before law? While a similar violation of law merits the same punishment, the rational approach requires each person's background, previous history, and context of the violation be given consideration to determine a fair punishment. So people cannot be accorded equality, either by pay, service, or treatment.

We could respond that if we scrutinized beyond the person and living beings, all constituents of matter are equal as the laws of physics spare not the tiniest particle and every particle in the universe is acted upon equally without discrimination. But it is a dissatisfactory resolution as the spirit of equality is felt to be among us – living, breathing, exploratory creatures.

Is equality merely a ghost principle – non-existent, one agreed to unthinkingly with no pragmatic utility?

To gain an appreciable understanding, we can muse over a particular chapter of the Hindu epic the Mahabharata. It describes the tumultuous times in India as the rising antagonism between cousins and rival claimants to the throne culminated in the battle at Kurukshetra. Before battle, Krishna, regarded as the incarnation of the Supreme Deity, agreed to side with the Pandava princes – those fighting for the righteous cause – on the condition that he be a charioteer and pick up no arms. His army meanwhile would fight on the opposing side – the Kauravas.

That a king be part of battle as a mere charioteer was unthinkable, but he did so, and fulfilled the role dutifully. It was a mark of humility of the one who had grown up in humble circumstances.

Were we to revisit a characteristic of the ego, the ego is what creates superiority and inferiority, as a survival measure. While the performance of duties in a given role is simply dharma, so all power, or privileges granted one for his role and exercised *only* for that role are not assertions of the ego. Whereas actions taken out of a personal interest that use privileges of one's role become so.

Then that which is truly equal is as exemplified by the example of Krishna – it is where every role is equal, has its own importance and dignity; and he who seeks what is perceived as a coveted role must see all roles as essentially equal, and be willing to take up any if so needed.

Any action taken in the fulfillment of one's dharma is free of all repercussions. But those that come from the ego are unequal, bound by pride, and so are doomed to the corresponding reactions of karma.

And I return to the age I am brought to. The various ages of the world are as different facets of a gem – they may shine and scatter light differently, but glint and gleam in their own way and their summation constitutes the whole gem. This age is as the others, but the only one where humans are at the point their decisions affect the whole planet. Never has it been so in history. Even when large armies fought before, their impact was minuscule and affected only a small region.

Only in this age has the population come to the level that manufacturing goods for the people has begun to change the composition of the basic elements of life – the surrounding air, water, and land. Technology, too, is at that mark as to modify the planet beyond recognition. Nuclear war can have the world submerged in radiation practically instantaneously. Artificial intelligence can make thralls of us all and keep us so unless properly understood and monitored.

To the man who has lived unaware, oblivious to the real dangers of the age, it may be unlikely and remote – ludicrous – and it always seems so until it happens. One can never underestimate the magnitude of human stupidity.

We are cast onto a blue green world bobbing gently in space around a fiery star, brought into life and being, in the most decisive time: either to be part of the grand triumph of technology and the human spirit – to rise, and soar well beyond anything our ancestors had even dreamed of, to spread out to the stars to the eager dawn of a Galactic Age. Or to fall, to plunge far into the deepest pits of despair and ignominy knowing the potential that could have been and being haplessly impotent to achieve it, impeded by the intransigence of the ego.

The resources of this world are not inexhaustible, but the stir of desires for every attractive new item or preparation may be endless. Giving them importance is a trick of the ego, which assigns value to transient material. Its indulgence may satiate one, though only temporarily. To live by dharma allows one to pierce through the silliness of fluctuating wants, to pull one from the sea of desire that removes the veil of ego over the eyes. When one sees sudden impulses and abrupt needs as just that – bubbles of feeling and thoughts that float and wander past, that can simply be watched and let by unhindered.

The immortal truth may be reached at by the delicate steering of dharma – a touch of the divine to forge a path where otherwise none could be found. Dharma is to forego the individual ego and gain a collective awareness – the fundamental unity of all living beings, the harmony of nature. Its observance provides a route to the cusp of a new world which in its magnificence, its sheer subtlety, is stranger, more miraculous and far more wonderful than could ever be imagined.

The End